From Sailor to Saint
How I Found True Peace and Happiness

PRAISE FOR
FROM SAILOR TO SAINT

Your book touched me so much! It's interesting and thought-provoking. I want my son to read this book. Keep doing what you're doing.

PATRICIA JAMES
ENTREPRENEUR/HOMEMAKER

Your story is very compelling. It is reader-friendly, accessible, warm, and personal. As a narrator, you are engaging and sympathetic and the reader is quite interested to hear your story in its totality!

ROBERTA TENNANT, MA
EDITOR-IN-CHIEF, FALCON BOOKS

My son's book is worth the read. I'm very proud of him and encourage every mother to have their children digest Randrick's message. My son is changing the world. He is dedicated to helping the poor and oppressed find physical and spiritual relief – both in the US and around the world. I love you son. Keep up the good works.

CLAUDIA K. CHANCE
PROUD MOTHER OF THE AUTHOR

In Sailor to Saint, Randrick Chance takes the reader on an exciting adventure from searching the endless seas of emptiness to the safe harbor of joy, purpose and contentment. His search for fulfillment is recounted in a personable and engaging manner that draws the reader to the Source of all fulfillment: Jesus Christ. All who read it are sure to be blessed and filled with hope. I enthusiastically and wholeheartedly recommend this book.

MARTIN C. HODNETT, PSYD.
PROFESSOR, OAKWOOD UNIVERISTY

Randrick Chance is proof positive that God is still in the business of evangelism and soul winning! Randrick is infected with the virus we all need. He experienced God's transforming power. Now he can infect everyone he comes in contact with. You'll catch the same fervor that drove all the great soul winners as you read this book.

LEO SCHREVEN
PRESIDENT, ALL POWER MINISTRIES

From Sailor to Saint

How I Found True Peace and Happiness

RANDRICK CHANCE

7th Seal
MISSIONS RESOURCES
Huntsville, Alabama
www.7smr.org

7th Seal Missions Resources, Inc.
P.O. Box 11942
Huntsville, AL 35814
www.7smr.org

All Bible Quotations, unless otherwise stated, are taken from the King James Version (KJV). Italics not found in original quotations are used for emphasis. (Parentheses) denote supplied words or explanation.

ISBN - 13: 978-0-9843951-4-9
ISBN - 10: 0-9843951-4-8

Printed in the United States of America.

Cover Design: Randrick Chance & Kimberly Artis
www.artiskim.com

This book is dedicated to the men and women of the U.S. Armed Forces, who valiantly lay down their lives daily to defend our nation's freedom and preserve democracy around the world. Thank you.

And

to you,
for sharing this journey with me.

All proceeds from this book are for supporting dedicated missionaries and young people in fulfilling the Great Commission in the United States and around the world.

CONTENTS

Preface

I Paul, an apostle (not of men, neither by man), but by Jesus Christ, and God the father, who raised Him from the dead, do hereby certify this Randrick Chance that the Gospel he is preaching to you is not of man. For he neither received it of man, neither was he taught it, but by the revelation of Jesus Christ Himself.

You will look into his past life and may be quick to pass judgment but know this — it pleased God to call this young man even before he was born to be saved by grace. To reveal Jesus to him that he might now preach this same Jesus to the world boldly. Straightway, he did not confer with flesh and blood whether he should do this or not but immediately left all to follow in the ministry.

God did not call him to the same route as other ministers so he is no ordinary preacher (as me). Choosing to obey God rather than man, Randrick's message is profound, showing that he is not ashamed of the gospel of Christ, for it is the power of God unto salvation to everyone who believes, to Christians first, and also to unbelievers.

Apostle Paul,
Servant & Prisoner of Jesus Christ,
Chief of Sinners — Turned Saint

Acknowledgement

I first give thanks to Almighty God for being so loving and patient and for His guidance throughout my life. Special thanks to my darling wife who has sacrificed so much in following the Lord. I have such great appreciation and admiration for the godly character you posses. This could not be possible without your loving support. *Te amo mucho.*

I also thank the following for their positive impact on my life: my precious parents -- Claudia Chance and Anselma Cupid. Pastors: Jaime Panton, Peter Baptiste, Edward Lluberes, Doug Batchelor, Brian McMahon, Brent Brusett, and Dr. Samuel Koranteng-Pimpim. Singer and Evangelist Derrick Hall. Captains: James Vitha, Thomas Buterbaugh, and David Zusi. Lieutenants: Thomas M. Bui, Lisa Hurdle, and Jeffrey Sandin. Chief Warrant Officer Wilfredo Orozco. Senior Chief Petty Officers: Connie Elliot and William Villanueva. Dr. Oliver Miller, Dr. Anthony Paul, Dr. Alan Parker, Kevin and Ambrozine Trent, Miguel Carmona, Lester Rogers, and Iphil Victory.

Introduction

Thank you for reading this book. I guarantee you'll be satisfied. Before we begin our adventure, I want to get our friendship off to a great start by filling you in on a couple of things. First, you will notice several acronyms used sometimes without explanation. When referring to people, I often refer to them by their rank initials and/or last names only. For example, SK1 refers to a Store Keeper First Class in the U.S. Navy and LT means Lieutenant. Do not let these little things trouble you, simply acknowledge the name and continue reading.

Secondly, this is not an autobiography. The essence of this work is to convey a message and move rather quickly to get to the main point. Where it was necessary to provide background information, I did so sparingly to get to the essentials. My history is not the focus of this book as I am still a young man with a long learning curve ahead of me. However, follow me along the paths of my life to discover true life purpose.

Lastly, I want to explain the term saint. Many people misconstrue this term to identify a title but this is not the case. Biblically, a saint is a godly person or God's people (saints plural). According to Easton Bible Dictionary, a saint is someone separated from the world and consecrated to God; one holy by profession and by covenant; a believer in Christ. (See Psalm 16:3; Romans 1:7; 8:27; Philippians 1:1; Hebrews 6:10).

We will stick to this definition for the purpose of this book. I am not trying to call my self a "holier-than-thou" or "perfect" in any way. Easton Bible Dictionary also states, "The word saint was not used as a distinctive title of the apostles and evangelists and of 'spiritual nobility' until the fourth century. In that sense, it is not a scriptural title." Please see the following texts below to understand the context of the word saint. It is a pleasure to share this message with you. Fasten your seat belts, enjoy your reading, and I will see you at the end.

SAMPLE USAGE OF "SAINTS"

Acts 26:10 Which thing I also did in Jerusalem: and many of the *saints* did I shut up in prison, having received authority from the chief priests; and when they were put to death, I gave my voice against them.

Romans 1:7 To all that be in Rome, beloved of God, called to be *saints*: Grace to you and peace from God our Father, and the Lord Jesus Christ.

Romans 8:27 And he that searcheth the hearts knoweth what is the mind of the Spirit, because he maketh intercession for the *saints* according to the will of God.

1 Corinthians 6:2 Do you not know that the *saints* shall judge the world? and if the world shall be judged by you, are ye unworthy to judge the smallest matters?

Ephesians 2:19 Now therefore ye are no more strangers and foreigners, but fellow citizens with the *saints*, and of the household of God;

Philippians 1:1 Paul and Timotheus, the servants of Jesus Christ, to all the *saints* in Christ Jesus which are at Philippi, with the bishops and deacons:

Revelation 14:12 Here is the patience of the *saints*: here are they that keep the commandments of God and the faith of Jesus.

Chapter 1

The Early Days

I've always enjoyed life in the tropics because it is absolutely exciting and carefree, with approximately 500 miles of culture, history, and white sand surrounded by crystal clear blue water. Gems of the Lesser Antilles, St. Vincent and Grenadines are paradise retreats during winter months for people all around the world with an average temperature of eighty-one degrees year round. St. Vincent and the Grenadines are beautiful islands in the Caribbean –the place of my birth and upbringing.

St. Vincent is known by natives as "Land of the Blessed" and is deeply rooted with religious belief. From my earliest recollections, I've always been taught good values and biblical principles. My mother, Claudia

Chance, made sure our family attended church roughly five times per week because that's what she learned from her mother, Louise Chance. As a child, I even caught a "good-licking" if I missed church. There was Sunday morning and Sunday night services, Tuesday night Men's Fellowship, Wednesday night prayer meeting and Bible study, Friday night Women's Fellowship, and Saturday evening Youth Fellowship. I loved our little village Baptist church, even though we only had about thirty to fifty members in regular attendance. We often had a new pastor every two to three years so most of the elders would run the church.

Several missionary families often came to the little white church to hold Vacation Bible School (VBS), Dramas, Revival meetings and the like. It was in fact at VBS where I grew fond of the Bible and wanted to learn so much. I'm not sure if I was motivated by the various gifts the teachers gave for knowing the right answers but a seed was planted in my young heart for God's Holy Scriptures.

I vividly remember this old man, about eighty-five to ninety years old, who came to our church to hold a weekly series of meetings. It was here that I first heard the story of Pilgrim's Progress. All the youth were so enthralled that we would talk of it for days. What struck me most about our visiting friend was his incredible ability to memorize the Bible. This man actually memorized the entire Bible! He would say to the congregation, "Call out a scripture from anywhere in the Bible, and I will recite it." Most of the people called out some hard texts from the Old Testament, like Deuteronomy, but this lanky, old white fellow would rattle text after text — verbatim. "That's incredible!" I thought to myself. "I'd like to be able to do that."

After every service, there always seemed to be an altar call for baptism. At the early age of twelve, while in high school, I was first baptized by one of my favorite missionary pastors. Three of my cousins and some friends were baptized early one Sunday morning at the beautiful Villa beach, not too far from the main airport. It was a beautiful ceremony where the saints sang these old Negro spirituals as you came up out of the water. When the last candidate was baptized by the pastor, everyone received a certificate and was officially welcomed into the church as members.

Soon after, I was given opportunities to practice preaching at our Men's Fellowship services and I would also witness to my friends in the village and at school. My knowledge of scripture became extensive in a short period of time because I would spend hours memorizing Bible texts. Local churches on the island regularly competed with each other in Bible-bowls. I recall being one of the youngest on our team. Even at school, I was able to be on the Inter-School Christian Fellowship (ISCF) Bible bowl team. I took things so personally that even if we'd placed second, I would cry. Yes, cry (if you can imagine me crying).

In the Caribbean, children start school at a very early age. I graduated from high school at sixteen. At this time, I was trying to figure out what to do with my life. Since my father was in the U.S.A, he decided to send for us to live with him in Merrillville, Indiana. I had never heard of Indiana before, so it was strange getting this message. In my mind, America was New York, California, Texas and Washington. I wasn't even aware there were so many states. I was excited because this was a lifetime dream of many young people who live in St. Vincent. The news was quickly heralded to all my friends and cousins. We would sit around for hours and envision what America would be like, with vivid imaginations creating our dream home, driving our dream car, and eating all of the delicious foods we saw on television.

On February 8, 1997, my brother and I left our homeland for a better land. We parted sadly but joyfully because we believed better things awaited us. The flight seemed to take a lifetime and the anticipation was overwhelming. Everything was a first for us. Oh those good old days! When we arrived at Chicago O'Hare International airport, we instantly noticed the change! As soon as we met the frigid climate, we wanted to head back to St. Vincent. It was freezing! Suddenly, we went from eighty-plus degree weather to sub-zero temperatures. A new phase in my life had begun for me on these chilling American shores.

Although I had dreamed of living in the U.S, my ultimate plan was to get a good collegiate education and return to St. Vincent to work for the government. I applied to Purdue University to pursue an engineering degree. When I learned that I would be unable to immediately attend Purdue due to my foreign student status, and that it would take a while to get my high school transcripts evaluated, I decided to enroll at Merrillville High School.

Chapter 2

Why Navy?

It was at Merrillville High School that I got my first taste of the U.S. military. Up to this point, it had never dawned on me to consider the military. I had no clue what the military was even about. After about a month there, I began noticing naval recruiter AG2 James Pollock. He always looked impressive in his Navy uniform. He was a sharp sailor! Visiting the recruiting table, one day, ignited a spark of curiosity and excitement about the U.S. Navy. As I listened and learned about the travel opportunities the Navy offered, I was hooked. I went home that day and read every piece of literature Recruiter Pollock had given me about a career in the Navy.

I showed them to my dad, and at first he was wondering why all of a sudden I wanted to join the military. I did the recruiter's sales pitch on him but he wasn't quite convinced. We then set an appointment for Petty Officer Pollock to come to our home and discuss "Why Navy?"

About a week later, Pollock visited my home to meet with my father and step-mother. We reviewed the information. Dad soon became proud of my decision and supported me. The Montgomery GI Bill was the major contributing factor in gaining my father's support for the Navy. He was also very impressed with Recruiter Pollock's appearance and mannerisms. He was "squared-away."

Dad gave me the final decision to make regarding joining the Navy. Why did he have to give me that choice? It was a done deal for me at this point. I already decided I was going to join the U.S. Navy. This sealed the decision. The next step now was to take the Armed Services Vocational Aptitude Battery test (ASVAB).

The Recruiting Office

I didn't take much time to prepare for the test because of the excitement, nor was I nervous, but calm and confident. The recruiter came to pick me up at the house and took me to the recruiting office to take the test. I went in the testing room and was elated that it was not difficult. AG2 Pollock did not even mention what I needed to score on the test to join the Navy, but I knew I had done well when we proceeded to sign additional papers. I scored a sixty-eight on the test and at that time, the minimum score for the Navy was thirty-one. You should have seen how proud my dad was when he knew I scored well above the minimum score.

Everything seemed to be going smoothly at this point, in fact, they were too smooth. Suddenly, I was thrown a curve ball. This was the first obstacle in joining the Navy — getting parental consent. Since I was only seventeen years old, I needed to have both parents' signatures to join the Navy and this caused some delay. All the other required documents were furnished to the recruiting office but this was a testing moment.

My mother was not too thrilled about the idea. She now lived in New York and she carried the typical fears that mothers have about their son joining the military. She was worried that I'd be sent to war somewhere and killed. I understood what she was going through and I tried my best to convince her otherwise but to no avail. Due to mom's reservations, I had to delay my entry into the Navy until my eighteenth birthday.

On September 15th, I went to the Military Entrance Processing Station (MEPS) in Chicago, Illinois, to complete my physical and finish processing. I must admit, I wasn't very confident during the entire processing at MEPS. Albeit, I was in good shape and good health, I was very nervous. It was the atmosphere of being among so many military people that terrified me. The long lines and waiting didn't help either. It felt like I was at the MEPS a year, just waiting and waiting for the next step. Even before I was in the Navy, I learned the phrase "hurry up and wait."

Recruiter Pollock was not close, so I was there all alone. My brain was going about one hundred miles per minute with many thoughts and my cranium was hot-to-the-touch. It was nerve racking! Nevertheless, late that afternoon, all was well because I was now standing with a group of young men and women reciting the oath of enlistment with an Army officer. It didn't matter what I went through all morning, I was now in the navy.

After I returned from processing as a sworn naval recruit, my father was so delighted and proud that he began shouting. I love him so much for that. It really made me feel good to see my father so proud of me. This moment was special for us; I was the first person in the family from the Caribbean to join the military. This entire time was amazing for me. Having planned to attend college and return to the Caribbean, I now was in the United States Navy, after only eight months in America. Eleven days after being sworn in at MEPS in Chicago, I was shipped off to begin basic training. I could not wait to begin this new era, desiring the real taste of military life.

Chapter 3

Basic Training

A few days prior to leaving, I got my acceptance letter from Purdue University and could begin registering for classes. My family wanted to know what I was going to do, since my transcripts were now evaluated and engineering seemed to be a good path to take. I thought about it a little but the Navy still seemed the best way to go. There was so much to look forward to and I couldn't turn back now. Respectfully, I told them the Navy was still my choice.

The morning of September 26, 1997, began an arduous day for me. After saying goodbye to my father and siblings the day before, I was off to the Ramada Inn to spend the night, before going back to MEPS for another brief physical and "swear-in" ceremony. That night I couldn't sleep too well because I was thinking about all that was before me. I drank a lot of water, did many push-ups, and prayed a lot. Before I knew it, we had to muster in the lobby for the bus to take us to MEPS, moments before dawn.

All went well at MEPS, though I was still somewhat unnerved. Once I was given my medical records, I knew this ordeal was over and it was now time to board the bus for boot camp at Great Lakes, Illinois.

Boot camp was a solid eight weeks of intense training. The days started at about 3:30 am through TAPS at 10:00 pm (Lights out). They taught us basic seamanship: firefighting and damage control, teamwork and communication skills, physical fitness, and discipline. After the first two weeks of training, all my fears had subsided and I was actually now enjoying Boot camp and Navy life. I liked the exercises and the strictness that were being instilled. Everything was in order and neat, and it made me feel good about myself. I never received many letters in Boot camp. But to this day, I am still anxious to receive mail and check my mailbox practically every day.

The news came that we were graduating in early December and my dear friend, I cannot begin to tell you how relieved I felt. The Great Lakes area was just too cold! (I cannot stand cold weather even today). This was torture for me you must understand. I remembered this particular day in November it snowed and I had "Snow-Detail." We had to go outside and shovel the snow. Oh, it was atrocious! I had never experienced the cold like this before. During that time, we rotated watch every twenty minutes or so and after my first watch, I did not make myself accessible for another watch.

Soon it was time for graduation pass-in review and my dad was present. As usual, he exhibited pride in his boy. On December 5, 1997, I was now ready for phase two of my training, "A" School held at Naval Technical Training Center (NTTC) in Meridian, Mississippi. For about six weeks, I learned to perform my job in supply and logistics. Again, we were held to high standards and exercised rigorously. By this time, I had even more self-discipline and devoted my time to study and excellence.

In our class, they explained a program called Accelerated Advancement Program (AAP), where the top graduate was given the option to be promoted to the next higher rank and on to Petty Officer Third Class (E-4). The recipient had to extend their naval service one year. That grabbed my attention and I made up my mind that I would be in that category. During "A" school, I never went to parties, but did what I was supposed to do and studied every day. I started out at the very bottom, as a Seaman Recruit (E-1) but determined to be the very best in the Navy and move up in rank quickly. If I were going to be a sailor then I would be the best Sailor possible. When it came time to graduate, all the students were given several options of where they wanted to be stationed.

My Options were the USS Abraham Lincoln in Washington and the USS Frank Cable AS-40 (a submarine tender) in Apra Harbor, Guam. Naturally, I wanted to go overseas where it was tropical, so I picked Guam without hesitation. This made me very excited and I looked forward to my first duty station.

I also managed to graduate from "A" School as the AAP recipient and was automatically promoted to

Seaman Apprentice (E-2) with promotion to Petty Office Third Class (E-4) pending completion of a few Personnel Qualification Standards (PQS). On February 8, 1998, I was headed to the airport to fly to Guam. Now the journey had really begun.

Chapter 4

Let the Journey Begin!

The moment I got on that plane to Guam, I was excited, ready to explode. Here I am, an island kid from St. Vincent, now on the complete opposite side of the world! Just the thought of that was ecstatic. I was already traveling the world, all free and loving every minute of it!

The flight to Guam was a long one and we had to pass through Hawaii first. I remember as the plane was landing on the soil of Hawaii how visually appealing was the aerial view. I could literally see the coral reefs and verdant sea floor from hundreds of feet above. When we landed, there were greeters in the airport with flowers and signs reading "Aloha Hawaii." I wanted to stay there, I mean, why go any further? Change my orders to any naval installation on Hawaii, I was in paradise. Well, I was not that fortunate but I had no idea what was in store for me in Guam because it was equally gorgeous and would become my home for the next two years.

About seven hours after we had re-boarded the plane, I was again breath-stricken with beauty and splendor as we descended on Guam International airport. I am actually reliving the experience right now as I write. After clearing my bags, I went curbside and there was already a Navy shuttle bus waiting, so we headed straight for the ship. A thousand thoughts ran through my mind on the way to the ship.

Although it was dark, Guam seemed like a lovely place to live. The duty-driver was explaining all about the ship, places to eat and have fun, and what Navy life was like on Guam. When I got to the ship, I was assigned a rack in the supply berthing because the ship was undergoing repairs and most of the sailors had moved off the ship to base housing. This was an interesting time for me I must admit. The rack was like a coffin. Just enough space to turn over slightly. They were built like bunks with very little headspace. I cannot begin to tell you how many times I bumped my head on the rack above me during those first days aboard ship. Later, I was wise enough to only choose the top racks. They had more room for maneuvering and I could even sit up straight in my rack. I had to be careful with the overhead pipes though, but they were my friends because I used them for storage.

I had to learn so many things when I first joined the Navy since I was still new to American living. One of the things I felt so ashamed of (through no fault of my own) was my inability to drive a vehicle. Oh, this was a thorn in my side. Everyone else (it seemed) was driving and here I am, eighteen years old and had never driven a car. It became my personal quest to get a drivers license. When I went out with people, I always came up with excuses for why I did not want to drive, all of which was only to hide my inadequacy.

I called a local driving school and started taking some classes. I never told anyone where or what I was doing when I went to classes. I did not even have to take the full theory portion of the class because I told the instructor I did not have much time and needed my license before deployments.

Once I got the certificate, I went to register for the drivers test at Guam DMV. Since I was not ready, I used the permit for some practice. I got my friend Andrés to give me some lessons. He was the only person I could trust with my "secret flaw" because he was a fellow islander from Martinique and a brilliant young man who spoke four languages fluently. The way I overcame this dilemma was by renting cars for about three weeks and having Andrés as my instructor.

I remember one afternoon in particular waiting anxiously on the ship for him to come and take me to practice. My blood was boiling hot and thick that day as my patience ran thin. "Where is this man with my rental?" I angrily thought. When he finally showed up, I couldn't even utter the words of frustration. But off driving we went.

Just before the test, I went on the road with an instructor for $60.00 and he said I could use his car for the test. I didn't care how much it cost to get my license; therefore, renting wasn't a problem. I never rented regular cheap cars but mostly two-door sports cars. Finally the day came for me to take the test and I had a full day's work lined up so I asked my supervisor for a few hours off. He gave it to me but I never told him exactly where I was going. The instructor came to pick me up and off to DMV we went.

After signing-in and waiting a little, an old man came and called my name. He was my examiner! We pulled out of the DMV and went on the highway. I did everything correctly and even did my parallel parking smoothly. Why then was I surprised when I got back in front of the DMV and the examiner told me, "You failed!" I could have died! "What do you mean I failed?" I asked. He replied, "You were too scared to get out into the traffic from the last intersection." What a reason to fail someone!

I did take a while to get from the intersection but that was because I did not want to appear too aggressive, I was treading softly. What a bitter disappointment. I had to take time away from work to take this test and he failed me, for one silly reason. I didn't let that stop me, however, so I registered for the test the following week. This time I rented a car and took Andrés with me. I had to ask for time off again so I gave my supervisor a good excuse and was on my way. (I was an excellent worker and my division knew it so it was not a problem getting time off.)

I signed in again and waited just a little while. This time my examiner was a younger gentleman, a military veteran. Perfect. He set me at ease right away. "Just drive," he said, and drive I did. We talked about military stuff all the while I drove the assigned route. I came to the parking lot and did my parallel park. He looked at me and said, "You've got your license." With joy unspeakable, I said to myself, "Praise the Lord!" Up to that point, I felt like that was the biggest accomplishment of my life. I called my step-mom and told her I had my license and she was happy for me.

I went back to work that day with a driver's license, proud, head held high, mission accomplished. I just could not stop looking at my license picture; no more hiding, I had my credentials to drive now and there was no holding back.

Since I had a valid driver's license, I needed a car, so I started hunting for one. My best friend Paul (as we were driving one day) saw a nice car parked along the road in Tamuning for sale. We stopped and went to check it out. Paul knew everything about cars, he lived for cars and he recommended I buy it. It was a Nissan Maxima in mint condition for only $4,900.00. I went to my Credit Union to get a loan but since I had no credit at this time they started me out with $4,500.00. With that approval, I called the seller, negotiated, and she agreed to sell it for $4,500. I drove away with my first car. No one could touch me now. Not only did I have my driver's license, I had my own car too.

Paul and Mary (now his wife) were excited for me and we all drove in my new wheels together. They made me nervous though because Mary would often get scared at my driving. To remedy this, I drove solo for the next few months until I felt I had a handle on things and soon began drawing attention to myself. I saved some money and bought some new chrome rims for my ride and skulls for the tire valves. This immediately made my car immaculate and people wanted to buy it. Even Mary's sister offered me $7,200.00 for it! A good offer but I could not give up my car for anything.

This set the tone for a downward spiritual spiral. My work never seemed to be affected with my lifestyle for some reason. On the job I would be "AJ" squared away and spoke with military decorum but off duty I whipped this tongue like a true sailor. My first priority was to move to the top in the Navy quickly and I made sure there was no error in my work. I was assigned seven storerooms as a Seaman Apprentice. My evaluations were always "4.0/Early-promote" and within my first four months as a brand new sailor, I was promoted to Petty Officer Third Class (PO3). This required a one year extension of service, but it was well worth it to me.

This promotion commanded respect among my peers and I felt very proud about it. From my early days in the islands, I always had older friends because it was the smart thing to do. I figured if I was on par with my older peers then my cohorts would have some catching up to do. It's like having the competitor's edge. I had a more supervisory role now and dispatched my duties with even more exactness.

Next, I set my sights on the coveted Enlisted Surface Warfare Specialist pin (ESWS) and qualified for it as a third class petty officer. At this time, it was a requirement aboard Navy ships for senior enlisted personnel to have the ESWS pin for promotion and so it was very important for me to get that pin.

Shortly after this achievement, I was promoted to Petty Officer Second Class (E-5). I was the youngest Second Class Petty Officer aboard my ship at the time of that promotion. My girlfriend at the time was mad at me because I ignored her while preparing for advancement exams. But I knew I must get to the top as fast as possible and nothing was to stand in my way (except myself).

With all these things going well for me, I felt satisfied with myself in the Navy. I had my license, a nice car, a beautiful island girlfriend, an impressive service record, played soccer for the ship's team, and had money in the bank. Before I joined the Navy, I had set a goal of saving $20,000.00 by the end of my enlistment contract. Several guys in our supply berthing would even borrow money from me, married guys especially.

It was never a problem to loan it to them. All I had to pay was car insurance and my loan and that was very feasible so I had everything under control. Because I was too young to drink in Japan, whenever we went there for ship repairs, I would study and take a few college courses. However, when we got back to Guam it was a completely different picture.

Every weekend I found myself at the club. I started as a shy person in the clubs. After a few months I only needed a little alcohol to get in the "groove." Although I would only drink on weekends, I always had to have a "long island ice-tea" to loosen up so I could enjoy myself. By this time I could not trust women. It really surprised me how women in this part of the world seemed to carry themselves and what their values were. It looked like everyone was trading partners like it wasn't a problem.

Soon it was normal for me as well and I became leery of any woman that wanted me to be her boyfriend. I would rather just have fun than claim anyone for my personal girlfriend. Until I met my wife, there was only one person I knew who was the exception to this rule, a local island Chamorro. It was even a woman that gave me my first puff on a cigar! I could never stand smoking and am thankful I was not hooked on that one. I tried cigars three times but detested it!

This was all there was to my life now. It was a set routine, almost automatic. I was programmed. I had Navy living down-packed, my career was stable, and I was having fun. Besides work, what else could I be lacking? I was on vacation and Guam was my paradise. *Or so I thought.*

Chapter 5

The First Encounter

The values I was inculcated with at a young age began to wane and only my mother seemed to slip in a little religious stuff here and there when she wrote or when we talked on the phone. Those childhood teachings were still there but somehow I fought persistently to "still" that inner voice. My first real encounter with biblical substance came one afternoon in December, 1999, aboard the U.S.S. Frank Cable while on duty. Tired that afternoon after my watch, I retired to the male berthing area browsing through the magazine rack, looking for something to read just to kill some time.

Since I was into other things, it was surprising to me when I chanced upon an Amazing Facts Bible study guide. The title of the study was startling. I was compelled to pick it up and read. I had never heard the name of this Christian ministry before and it sounded so unique. This was the beginning of an adventure into discovering God in a completely new way. The rest of the day was spent going through that study lesson as it was interestingly exciting. Since it was part of a correspondence course, I mailed in the study and couldn't wait to get the next lesson. From this point, I really began taking an interest in spiritual things. After this first lesson, I began reading the Bible sporadically on my own in a brand new way.

I remember one of my shipmates (HT3 Beau) was trying to witness to me during these times. He invited me to church several times and I went, though often unwillingly. The church was at the University of Guam and I was involved in several activities and found it quite interesting but my behavior was not altered. I would go to church now and again but still go partying at the same time.

As it came near the end of my tour, it was time to pick orders. I began searching once more for overseas assignments, since I liked the overseas billets. When I discovered Italy was open, I searched no further but immediately applied. Within a week, my orders were written for Naples, Italy, but they were cancelled two weeks later. It was not a devastating blow since there was an alternate duty station -- Naval Air Station Sigonella, Sicily. That pleased me just the same, so I took the billet.

My transfer date was March 2000 and since I had not taken leave for two years, I accumulated many vacation days on the books and money in my pocket. So I decided to go visit my parents before I went to Italy. At the end of my tour, the supply department awarded me Sailor of the Quarter and my first Navy Achievement medal. I also earned a great evaluation and recommendation for early-promote (advancement).

Before leaving Guam, I sold my car for $6,500.00 to a good African friend of mine because he deserved it and I could always get a ride if I needed. For the last day on the island I rented a white convertible Camero and with Paul, Mary, and my girlfriend, we went around the island, took many pictures, laughed and even cried together as free young people enjoying life to the fullest. It was such a blast.

One of the challenging things about Navy life was leaving good friends whom I had spent a few years getting to know and then having to start all over again in a new location. As for the Bible study guides I encountered earlier in Guam, all was not lost. I would eventually continue with the lessons (stay tuned for more on this life-transforming journey).

I went home on leave to Indiana and had a great time. Now that I was back, my brother and friends seemed to think I had the world of money and so I was paying for almost everything. I've always found it interesting how this seems to be the case with friends. Not that I was complaining because I thought I was the man now and felt good actually being the spender. I bought us both nice leather jackets, paid for the drinks, movies, and even gas. Overall, I enjoyed my time together with them.

Dad seemed quite calm with my new changes and did not give me a hard time even with both ears pierced. I think he might have flipped the switch though if I came home with tattoos. I'm glad I didn't go for that one either. However, the night before my flight to Italy, my dad was upset with us. I had gone to the club with my brother and his friends in East Chicago and did not get home until a few hours before my flight that early morning. Dad drove to the airport and the family came to say goodbye which really meant the world to me. We took some real goofy pictures but it was a good way to be shipped off again.

It was yet another long flight to endure but I was excited because this was a completely new journey and different culture. I was going to wine and dine with fine Italian cuisine (I especially loved Italian bread) and visit Rome, Malta, Milan, and other historic places.

Chapter 6

The Journey Continues

My flight was delayed several times so when I landed at Catania airport, my sponsor was not there to pick me up. Moreover, my entire luggage did not make it with me. There was a shuttle waiting to take people to the base so I was dropped off at the air terminal. Since I was assigned to the Air Cargo division, the Airman on watch called my sponsor to meet me at the terminal. Within ten minutes, SK2 Ringaman came and took me in her car to my Temporary Lodging Apartment (TLA). She took me back to the airport several times and I got my luggage a day or so later.

I faced another obstacle early in Sicily. Most vehicles in Italy are manual transmission and I could not drive stick shift. Many times I thought to myself, "Why did I sell my car?" I was entitled to a rental but all they had were stick shifts. It was almost like being back at square one again. However, one of my coworkers, SK3 Figueroa, offered to teach me so I rented my first of many cars in Italy. I was thrilled about having him teach me because he was a simple and patient guy. I actually learned to handle the gears within an hour. It took me a while to get the feel of things but I had the basics down-packed so I was ready to go.

One of the ploys thrown my way was having my TLA right beside the night club. Just what I needed. My first weekend there, I went on base across from my apartment and I met James who would become my best friend in Italy and one of my best friends for life. James and I clicked automatically. He was an Aviation Machinist's Mate (AD) and worked in a different department but on the same flight line. He stayed in the barracks and we just seemed to have so much in common. James grew up in Africa, Kenya to be exact, and loved reggae music (also my favorite at the time) so we were listening to music in his room as we got acquainted. We were like brothers -- partying together and looking out for each other. Nothing separated us. In fact, as far as I can recall, James and I never had an argument.

I didn't stay in the apartment long because the music was annoying at night and my TLA privileges were running out. I found a wonderful place not too far from the base at Via Risorgimento N.15/A, Motta San Anastasia. I could not believe it, my own apartment, and my own space — could Navy life be any better? This was a big step up from the confined spaces on a ship. Now I had two full bedrooms, a large kitchen, and living room, all for one person. Promotion really pays. Only Petty Officer Second Classes and above or sailors with dependents had their own housing so I really got a chip on my shoulder for this freedom and luxury.

Next it was time to get another car. As I was driving one day I noticed a "for sale" sign on a BMW and it caught my attention. I called the owner and he was happy to show it to me. Joe Nicolosi kept his BMW in great condition. He did not have to sell me on the car. I sold myself! It was a white BMW-520I, lovely interior, good sounds, and manual transmission. It was a done deal. This however, continued my downward spiritual spiral. That BMW did more for me than I was willing for it to do. I was drawing attention once more. (Notice the pattern, repetition, and sequence of events). Life couldn't be any better than this.

Outwardly I seemed fulfilled, happy, and in control but deep inside I felt miserable and without a definite purpose. I even came to despise the very things I thought brought me contentment and felt so alone. How could someone like me, who had what most young people wanted, be so lonely inside? Beneath the mask, I was really a shy and insecure person.

Chapter 7

The Enemy and His Traps

When you take time to examine your life and just be still to observe your life in detail, you will notice there seems to be a battle between the forces of good and evil. It is a controversy between Jesus and the enemy, Satan. And like it or not, the prize is your soul and life. It should then come as no surprise that the devil uses every deception to keep us in darkness and stop us from obtaining eternal life. When I carefully considered my lifestyle, I saw clearly this cosmic warfare being played out before my eyes. In short, I was caught in the schemes of Satan and enslaved to the passions of my flesh. I had fallen into the "rat-race" of life, the misconceptions many people now find themselves having. Here is what the enemy's traps looked like in my life.

Every weekend found me in the night clubs. Partying like there was no tomorrow. My self worth was found in dating the prettiest women, dressing in the trendiest clothes, and wearing expensive jewelry to impress the young ladies on the base. I figured this was the American life since it was the image projected by the music stars and entertainment industry. In Guam, I first came out of my shell when I got my first car and again, in Italy, I quickly attracted attention and gained popularity when I got my second car.

James and I, along with a few others, would rent luxury cars like Mercedes Benz, BMW, and Audi on the weekends and travel to Palermo (a great distance from the base) so we could party. Every week, the same routine: spending, drinking, and clubbing. What a waste of life! There was no time to stop, no time to think. I was automatically programmed to do these things. All the people I associated with at this time were doing the same things so why should there be any changes?

The enemy knew that having these kinds of influences would ensure I remained ensnared by his devices. I'm sure you have seen these things in your life as well. My idea of success was false. What really was success? It was all vanity and vexation of spirit! Within the seven years I had been in the Navy I went through seven cars. That equates to one car per year!

None of these things really brought me contentment. Absolutely nothing! All this only made my heart dark and hard. What disrespect I gave some of those ladies and sad, but true, what disrespect some of those women showed themselves. Yet this was all fun — wasting money and energy maintaining a front. Deep within I was insecure and introverted, looking for someone to rescue me from myself. It was all foolishness and exasperation of spirit!

This was seriously a heavy burden on my heart. The devil has millions of our young people chasing after the wind. Enslaving them to sexual immorality and financial bondage. These two taskmasters are destroying our lives and tearing down the very foundation of our society.

My reality became whatever was portrayed in the media. It was *OK* to have a few girlfriends, *OK* not to have commitment and even *OK* to disregard wise counsel. Not taking thought for the consequences of dysfunctional relationships, broken hearts, sexually transmitted diseases nor a negative bank account. Nothing seemed alarming. After all, payday was always just two weeks away. My icons became the rap stars and movie stars. Talk about chasing frivolous fantasies!

I began to see myself heading for destruction and ruin but was so overwhelmed in this lifestyle that I just could not seem to change. This was exactly where the enemy wanted me to be — destitute and broken. Are you beginning to see clearly the traps of the enemy?

The stars were wearing expensive jewelry and designer clothes so I thought this was the way to show you were rich. Therefore, I sought to buy the chains, watches, and clothes to play the role. Even though sometimes there was no money in the bank, no one knew about it. If you had expensive gear people assumed you had money somewhere.

The reality of the matter was, my friends and I were living paycheck to paycheck (like millions of Americans are today). One paycheck short of dead broke. But thanks to the regular Navy paycheck, things never quite fell apart.

I vividly remember one of the very first lessons my father taught me when I came to the United States was "never get a credit card." He explained to me why but I didn't pay much attention and since I didn't have a job at the time, it didn't stick. It took me three years after I joined the military to get my first credit card. When I did get a credit card to go on my first vacation from Italy back to Guam, I immediately maxed out the card. I had not even begun the vacation and I had reached my limit! Once again I had fallen prey to the enemy's trap. A snare that took another three years to break.

From then on, I began exploring ways to get rich quick. Even though I never sought illegal ways of becoming rich, my time was consumed searching the Internet for those get-rich-quick schemes. It just did not dawn on me that the only persons getting rich were the ones with the schemes. No wonder the Bible says that riches certainly make themselves wings and fly (Proverbs 23:5) because no matter what money-making scheme I tried, I just never made it big. It was like gambling. I wasted money in search of illusions and deceptions that hold our world spellbound by the sinister Satan.

Chapter 8

The Amazing Facts

We may not always see it, but even when we are buried in the world's philosophy of life and living as our own gods, the only true God of heaven is lovingly putting truth in our path. He encourages us to follow in the light we have at any particular moment. Light was penetrating my heart slowly but surely as I continued studying the Amazing Facts Bible study guides.

These lessons not only dealt in depth with Bible prophecy, they also covered various topics including: The Reliability of Scripture, The Origin of Sin and Satan, Salvation, Baptism, Heaven, Death, Hell, Christian Lifestyle, and The Immutability of God's Commandments. The latter subject on the lost day in history stirred within me a strong ray of light. These amazing facts presented in this lesson really caused me to think and to think very long and hard. I began to contemplate things now, questioning the teachings of many religions, including those I was taught while growing up. For the first time I was really thinking intellectually about spiritual things. Not just accepting my behavior by chance but also examining the behaviors of society as a whole.

Since we abided by the laws of society then we must abide by God's Laws as well. The laws of the land serve to protect us and keep us in line and likewise God's Ten Commandment Laws had to serve a similar purpose in guiding our lifestyles. I had never been taught the Law of God in this light before. The arsenal of Bible texts in that lesson made the facts irrefutable. How could I argue with almighty God? Moreover, I thought, Why am I trampling on His holy day every weekend? Why has the devil manipulated the world to do all the vile things on this blessed day of God as if it serves no purpose? Could so many people be deceived? Even well intentioned Christians? Could my own church from a youth have missed this vital point? What about the big preachers who "do away" with the commandments of God?

Are they really "nailed to the cross?" Could these clergymen be wrong? The truth was plain and God revealed it to me so I began to follow it.

I was convinced there was a better way to live and started getting my act together. I began attending a church about five minutes from my apartment in Motta and did not go to the night club for about six straight weeks. I was going to live right from then on. I continued the lessons by mail but took a longer time mailing them back for grading.

One of the hardest things was trying to live right in the same environment. I still hung out with the same friends and listened to the same music but I knew the clubbing was just not for me. There is a difference between being convinced and being convicted. I was convinced of truth but not convicted by truth. It had not sunk deep enough into my heart to cause a full conversion experience. Before I knew it, I was back in the midst again. Partying harder this time and pushing the envelope even further with my behavior.

I could all too well relate with the Apostle Paul. "O wretched man that I am! Who shall deliver me from the death of this body?" (Romans 7:24). The good I wanted to do was the good I did not do and the habits I hated were those I found myself doing. What a battle to win! I was my own enemy, caught on the devil's playground. Life continued as normal and though I read periodically, the blanket remained draped over my eyes so that I became desensitized to error.

My tour of duty was almost up in Italy and it was time once again to call my detailer for reassignment. Again I only desired overseas assignment so this time, I had my division chief call the detailer for negotiations. I wanted to go closer to my roots so she managed to get me assigned at Naval Station Roosevelt Roads, Puerto Rico. That was good news and I was looking forward to leaving Sigonella because I was tired of the same foolishness and wanted a fresh start.

To maximize the benefit of this assignment I had to re-enlist but that was fine with me because I would get to see another island. In November 2001, I re-enlisted for two years and was given a beautiful ceremony. My division officer LT. Sandin performed the ceremony and we were thousands of feet off the ground. My supervisor and I re-enlisted together in a helicopter while flying over Sicily. It was awesome!

Shortly before I transferred in March 2002, I

discovered I had a hernia and needed repair surgery as soon as possible. This put me on three weeks bed-rest, which I really enjoyed. Most of that time was spent at my good friend's home, AD2 Dickertone. He had his wife and mom take good care of me and it was during this time I also had some time to think. I would lie in the room and write poems about my life and release some frustrations that way.

Two weeks before my flight to Puerto Rico, the detailer called me and said he had to cancel my assignment on Roosevelt Roads because the Navy was considering closing that base (sounds familiar?). My household goods were already shipped; I had already sold my car and was ready to go. He told me, however, there was a billet at the recruiting processing station in San Juan and that it would be a good career move. It didn't matter because I was happy to be in the Caribbean and this cancellation was a blessing in disguise (as you will soon discover). I was entitled to Consecutive Overseas Tour (COT) privileges but I turned that down. There was no need to go anywhere, just get me to Puerto Rico, "la isla del encanto (the island of enchantment)."

Chapter 9

The Final Assignment

When I got to Military Entrance Processing Station (MEPS) San Juan, Puerto Rico, it was like going back to the recruiting office. Only it was much better this time. There were only four of us in the Navy office and all of senior rank: PN1 Garcia, who was the Leading Petty Officer (LPO), PN2 Brown, and SK2 Lluberes, whom I was to relieve in a few months. We worked well together but never mingled after work because PN1 and SK2 were married so naturally they went straight home at the end of a workday. I lived about an hour away from work and PN2 liked being by himself.

MEPS proved to be one of my biggest military blessings thus far. Thank God I had the chance to come here and leave all my friends behind. Since I was new to the island, I had no family nor friends to influence me, so naturally, I had a lot of time to focus on God and let Him work on my heart. I had time to think about where I was coming from and where I was going. Like many uninformed soldiers, I was so caught up in the vices of the devil and just could not focus on spiritual nor eternal things. I was temporarily blinded by these worldly delusions that many are trapped in today. Yes, I was trapped in the rat race (*but not for long*).

Soon it was time for PN1 to leave and PN2 was promoted, but he was retiring soon as well. SK2 was also promoted just before he transferred to his new billet in Jacksonville, Florida, so we had new personnel fill their spots. BMCS Villanueva came to fill retiring PN1 Brown's billet, PN1 Delgado and PN2 Postiglione also came aboard. Things changed considerably under this new leadership but the office became more efficient as a result.

I was still performing my duties in an exceptional manner. My duties included: interviewing, counseling, processing, and securing investigations for Navy applicants. Additionally, I took care of supplies and government vehicle maintenance. Because I was the first person to open the office when we had applicants on deck, I had to wake up at 3:30 am to get to the office no later than 5:30 am. This type of duty was mainly administrative and there was so much paper work involved. I learned most everything about Navy operation and regulations being stationed at MEPS. I found it interesting that I started my Navy career at MEPS and will finish it at MEPS.

I also had many vicissitudes in Puerto Rico, one being I had to move three times. The housing was great but I just was not settled and figured I needed new surroundings. What I really needed was a heart change. I began to sense my great need of God more than ever before and I knew He was working to set me free. During this time, I was ready to have him perform heart surgery and deal with my issues. It was a powerful life changing experience.

What happened next would forever alter the course of my life. I would never be the same man again. The word of God, through His holy scriptures, had taken root and was ready to germinate into a precious fruit, evidenced by a transformed life. The battlefield was leveled now and the oppressed saw clearly — there was a decided victory. The choice was mine to make, I had a part to play in determining who won the duel for my soul. It was a life and death decision, one of eternal consequence and it had taken years to achieve. Regardless, a new day was dawning on this sailor and a new day can dawn on you as well.

Chapter 10

The Conviction and Change

T his is where the reality of Jesus' power to change anyone became evident in my own life. No one can deny this power because I have seen, heard, and experienced it. As I continued soaking up the precious truths in each Bible study like a sponge, convictions grew deeper in my mind and heart. God was now speaking loudly and distinctly to me through His words and I could no longer quiet His voice. I couldn't stay on the sidelines a moment longer. Decision-time had come!

There were twenty-seven lessons in the study guide series and before I completed that last three, I resolutely took my stand for God to follow Jesus Christ as my Savior. I recognized my need for salvation. I realized that my sinful life caused Jesus to leave His throne and He died on Calvary to restore the breach and so I accepted His free gift of eternal restoration.

When I studied the lesson of God's call for His people to come out of corruption into his remnant fold (the church), I contacted Carolyn Moxley, an Amazing Facts representative, to ask her for the addresses of churches in Puerto Rico. She quickly and warmly responded and I began calling the numbers on the list. I could not get ahold of anyone at the Spanish churches so I called the local Christian radio station, WBMJ 1190, and they gave me the number for an English speaking church in my area.

I called the church office and one of the elders gave me directions and their worship hours. That same Sabbath, I went to the house of God to worship with His remnant people and it was like a glorious new beginning. I do not remember the sermon preached that day but I knew I was happy and at peace to be worshipping God on His Holy day and not at some club wasting time and life.

A few weeks later, the church had a week of revival

meetings and invited a dynamic preacher to deliver the nightly sermons. It turned out that the young preacher was also a Navy Veteran! He was a Religious Program Specialist — Third Class Petty Officer (RP3) and he too finished his active duty service obligation to become a soldier in God's army. Each night he delivered a very soul-piercing message. I did not miss one night!

Halfway through, I told the pastor of the church I wanted to be baptized. We went out to dinner and spoke about my decision to follow biblical truths. I shared with him my journey through studies with Amazing Facts Ministries (by this time I had completed all twenty-seven lessons) and was ready to make a public stand to join the body of Christ as a church member. He was satisfied with the examination and believed I was ready for this step.

On November 16, 2002, I was re-baptized and became a true disciple of Jesus and a part of His worldwide body of saints. It was a day of commitment and peace for me. My heart rested in God's assurance that I had indeed changed — from sailor to saint. I was a new Chance.

Now I wanted to share with everyone the miraculous deliverance God performed in my life. I wrote a letter and sent a copy of my baptismal certificate to Amazing Facts and they were filled with joy to have planted the seed that yielded fruit for Christ. I became alive and on fire for my God. Everything changed!

It has not been the same for me ever since I first picked up that lesson study aboard the USS Frank Cable AS-40. Today, I am still baffled as to how the study guide got aboard a naval vessel but ten thousand percent grateful that God can use small things to reach and confront complex people. He uses the simple and foolish things of this world to confound the (seemingly) wise and intellectual (1 Corinthians 1: 17-29).

God realigned my priorities. Now my desire is to do His will and share the good news of freedom and meaning found in knowing Jesus as Savior. My surrender to Him for service meant a whole lifestyle change. The earrings came out of my ears, the fancy jewelry was set aside, and I lost my appetite for ungodly music and entertainment. I literally cleaned house! CDs, DVDs and Videos went flying out of my apartment and car window. The process was not a lengthy one. God knew I had to have immediate victory and so He set me free from the things that once held me captive.

I am not a perfect man nor have I arrived at a place where I am no longer tempted to do wrong but I live daily for Christ and strive by His grace to be the man He destined me to become. To be on the safe side, I stopped watching television altogether. Throughout my tour in Puerto Rico, I never had cable and today I still do not have cable but the Idiot box sits in a corner, only to view Christian programs on DVD or video. Many evils no longer haunt me because the device is removed. The Bible says we must not make provisions for our flesh to gratify its sinful desires (Romans 13:14) and that's what I put into practice.

The devil has not stopped his assaults on my life but I look to Jesus to complete the work He has started in me (Philippians 1:6; Hebrews 11:2). This one thing I know, I am secure in Jesus Christ and have a personal relationship with Him. If I die today, I will rise to eternal life with Jesus Christ when He returns to earth the second time for all His saints.

More Evidences of a Changed Life

Most people cannot believe God by faith as the Bible teaches so they require tangible evidences. One of the most convincing evidences that the Bible is indeed inspired of God is the results of changed lives. God's Words transform people's lives like nothing else on this earth. It has done more for people than money, fame, prestige, and even health. Because of the biblical teachings of Scripture, drunkards have become sober, abusive parents become whole, victims find peace and restoration, thieves become honest and immoral people become pure and righteous (we could go on an on).

A few years earlier, I was controlled by the deceitfulness of worldly success and happiness. My idea of success and purpose was only about making a lot of money, driving expensive cars, dressing like a million dollars, and dating pretty women. How shallow and selfish! Fast forward seven years and now I stand a man transformed by the light of the world, Jesus Christ. It used to be that I could not be found close to a church, now I attend church faithfully. Almost every other word out of my mouth was a curse word, now my speech is seasoned with love and scripture. I now have no desire for weekend drinking and clubbing and my dress code now reflects the simplicity of Christian virtue.

My aspirations in life are to please my Heavenly Father and point men and women that are lost in the snares of this world to His son, Jesus Christ. My guiding principles are the sacred words of God found in His Holy Bible, not the traditions of men or the status quo of society. A close examination of before and after makes the evidence crystal clear, this man has experienced a radical transformation. Not just on the outside but more importantly, on the inside. It is because my heart has changed and my mind is set on heavenly things that the outward signs are visible. What you see on the outside is a testimony of the heart change on the inside. All thanks, praise, and glory is to almighty God.

I am set free and it was not because of any twelve-step program nor hypnotism but a direct result of allowing the Bible to penetrate my life and accepting the Lord Jesus Christ to be Lord of my life. It was the one-step plan. Weigh the facts before you and you will discover that Jesus is indeed the answer to a spiritually bankrupt world and life. The facts are present in my life that He does change, can change, and will change. This is not the same man most knew several years ago. As a result of my new life in Christ Jesus, I am now living with true purpose.

I first wrote this testimony as a letter to all my close

friends in December, 2002, to share with them both the problem and solution to a life of false pursuits. It then grew to fourteen pages (most of which are now included in this book) to bear the testimony of my conversion experience.

My coworkers took notice of the differences in my life and seemed puzzled for a while. I did not have to preach to them, they knew and respected my convictions. Also, my family, friends, and church noticed the zeal I had for living a godly life. So much so that the church members elected me to be their youth president and put me on their regular preaching schedule. Can you imagine that? A sailor preaching? You better believe it! God gave me something to say and I wanted to tell it to everyone, regardless of their acceptance.

My involvements in church activities were many: we did several outreach programs with our young people, organized a drama club, a men's mentoring group, an exercise program, and seminar presentations on finances. We even ministered to orphans and nursing homes in Puerto Rico. My focus had now changed from self to others. Why would I be reaching out to others on the weekends when I could have been at a night club somewhere? What changed? Jesus made all the difference!

Chapter 11

The Call is Heard

Like the prophet Isaiah, *"I heard the voice of the Lord saying, 'Whom shall I send? And who will go for us?' And I said, 'Here am I: Send me.'"* (Isaiah 6:8 — emphasis mine) Beyond the shadow of a doubt, God had something in mind for me that I never would have imagined. As my interests grew stronger and stronger in spiritual matters, my heart was experiencing even deeper conversions. On the way to work I would listen to the Christian radio station or play something godly on CD. I was not making any provisions for my flesh to fulfill its lusts. I began experiencing a burning desire to see young people set free from the things that captivated me. I became concerned about my family and friends' spiritual condition and what I could do to help. How could I share with my military family the dangers of spiritual bondage around them? Through the word of God — the Bible and my personal testimony, I wanted to reach out to young people.

While in Puerto Rico, news came from Italy about my friend James. He got into an accident and wrecked a brand new BMW and had to be rushed to Germany for immediate medical attention. My friend AD2 Dickertone sent me some pictures of James in a coma and I was shocked. I couldn't believe my eyes! In my sympathy for James, I pondered the implications. That could have been me in that vehicle with him because we went out together every weekend. I thought, "Does he know what I now know? What if he doesn't recover?" Praise God, he did recover but up to this day he has no recollection of the incident.

A few weeks later I got more news, this time from my homeland of St. Vincent. A good friend I grew up with was arrested and was now in prison! I asked myself, "What if I had warned both him and James earlier about that kind of lifestyle? What if I had shared my testimony earlier with them? What if they knew what I knew about the deceptions of the enemy? Then maybe... just maybe..."

It was clear that God was calling me to proclaim His message of freedom to the world, particularly His young people. I wondered long and hard how this would be possible. This scripture brought me hope and comfort: *"Forget the former things; do not dwell on the past. See, I am doing a new thing! Now it springs up; do you not perceive it? I am making a way in the desert and streams in the wasteland."* (Isaiah 43:18, 19 NIV)

The Amazing Facts College of Evangelism (AFCOE) was brought to my attention in one of their publications, the *Inside Report.* This program attracted me but the problem was getting enough vacation days to complete the training. Therefore, I put it on the back burner as just something to do in the future but I was constantly reminded of the AFCOE program by the magazine and the more I thought about it the more I wanted to do it, but how?

The Lord impressed me to leave the Navy upon completion of my active duty service obligation. He brought me the message wrapped in an unusual place aboard ship, now He wanted me to really forsake all and follow Him. It was a challenging decision. Many questions weighed so heavily on my heart I became depressed. "How would I support myself? Where will I get the money? The Navy is all I know."

I wanted to see the whole picture first. God, out of His loving mercy and understanding, provided answers in some remarkable ways. I proceeded to perform several tests to substantiate this decision. Albeit deep within my heart I wanted to be a witness and knew God wanted me to follow His high calling, I had every good reason (I thought) for staying Navy.

Chapter 12

The Call Confirmed

The next series of events that happened were more than compelling for me to follow God in this direction. While working on this decision, I continued serving at church faithfully and carrying out my military duties professionally. Dissatisfaction with my life and the church began to set in as I noticed some disturbing things around me. I saw many of the conditions I knew in the world among my people and that bothered me greatly. I even wondered if I was in the right church and decided to stay away for about one month to contemplate if this was indeed the place where God wanted me to be.

I prayed and fasted about it but soon knew that it was God's will for me to fellowship with the saints at church. This experience was a very humbling one because God showed me my own shortcomings and the need to be connected. With the changed attitude, I started to pray for change in the church. I read the book of Nehemiah and understood that the only time change comes is when our people repent of their backslidings. Armed with this knowledge, I began preparing a sermon to shed light on the issues.

I remember well that Friday evening when it came my turn to preach. I was downstairs in my apartment praying to God to change our hearts. I pleaded and confessed my sins and their sins and was in tears for quite some time as I poured out my petitions to a merciful Father. *I had never prayed like that before!*

For some reason beyond my comprehension, on the morning of the sermon, I couldn't print my notes from my home computer. I saved it on a disc and tried going to the office to print but the disc would not upload. My next option was to try at church but when I arrived and asked to get it printed, no one was able to print for me. What a dilemma — all that hard work and to no avail!

Either the enemy was trying to stop that message or God wanted me to rely completely on Him for power.

Knowing God, the latter was His will and understanding Satan, the former was his plot. I relayed the matter to our prayer ministry leader and we prayed. All I had were post-it notes in my Bible for the verses I was going to use. Having left the results to God, I went to the platform with the elders and awaited my turn to speak.

Before approaching the pulpit to preach, I prayed silently in my heart then proceeded to deliver God's message that day. I started out very slow and calm in my usual way. Then about halfway through the sermon, something miraculous happened. The Holy Spirit of God filled me and took over the entire message. *I never experienced anything like this before now.* My voice and expression changed and the words came out with such mighty power and authority. It was like standing outside myself and observing the action. The urgency of the message was so compelling, I broke down in tears — weeping as I called God's people to repentance and reformation.

Before the appeal (altar-call) was given, people were already standing. When I did make the call, everyone in the church came forward, except for three and they were standing in their seats (two of whom were also in tears). That served as a big confirmation to me because there is no greater joy than seeing people respond to God's call on their lives. I had seen what it was like from the pulpit and that planted a seed in my heart. Many people commented on that sermon and I couldn't take any credit at all. It was a powerful expression of God's might.

Shortly after this experience, I had to undergo another surgery in September, 2004, which put me on bed rest for a month. Though it seemed an inconvenience, it was during this time of recovery that my prayer and devotional life skyrocketed. I studied the Bible diligently, prayed and fasted earnestly to discover God's will and assignment for my life. This thorough soul-searching led me right back to AFCOE. It was the perfect training program to launch me into the battlefield for God. I came away from that mountain top reinvigorated — ready to follow the Master.

The next confirmation was in relation to this surgery and took place the following month when my friend Raul from Homestead, Florida, called me to ask if I would preach at a youth weekend event at his church. Though I was still healing and could barely walk, I accepted the invitation. I really didn't know what to preach but knew it would be a great opportunity.

I went to Florida on crutches to share with this group. Since I had written fourteen pages of my testimony, I asked Raul to print about seventy-five copies to distribute to the young people. They scheduled me to speak Friday night, Saturday morning, and Saturday evening. The night and morning messages went well but I felt like they didn't need any more sermonizing. What then would I talk about for closing that Saturday evening? I had not the slightest clue.

During the Sabbath lunch at Raul's, the thought came to mind to talk about my personal testimony with the youth. I had not planned to share it verbally but just gave it as a printed hand out. My message was very personal and curtailed to this audience. I shared with them most of what you're reading in this book up to that time. Many were touched by the words and shared their comments afterwards. One young man in particular came up to me and told me he really appreciated what I had to share and wanted me to come to his church and share the same presentation. I didn't quite know what it was but just the sincerity in his voice and eyes made a deep impression on me and that served as another confirmation.

Before I went back to work from convalescent leave, I made the decision to follow the call and go to Amazing Facts College of Evangelism. To make sure I didn't back out, I went ahead and applied (though the next session I applied for was almost a year off).

Once I got the application completed I thought I was on good ground. When I went back to the office, I started proclaiming my decision to separate from the Navy the following April. After a while I had to stop telling people about my decision because it was met with much negativity. They meant well but just couldn't understand my reasoning. The Bible says in 1 Corinthians 2:14, *"The natural man does not receive the things of God for they are foolishness to him. Neither can he know (understand) them because they are spiritually discerned."* Their feedback was discouraging and I questioned my decision even though I had enough confirmation.

Like Gideon, I proceeded to ask God for further evidence. To be one thousand percent sure, I asked the Lord for a tangible sign (thank God that He is so patient). By this time, promotion exams were underway, so I prayed to God and asked Him, "If you promote me to

Petty Officer first class (E6) then I would take this as a sign." This is not the general rule of thumb to know God's will but I think He winked at my immature faith. On the day of my exams, I simply prayed to God, told Him again about my decision if He promoted me, and I took the exam and forgot all about it.

God gave me a two-fold confirmation plan that was like a lightning bolt. On November 15, 2004, my Commanding Officer called the recruiting office and asked to speak with SK2 Chance (this was a rare thing). I answered the phone and he said, "Congratulations, SK2, you are now a first class Petty Officer in the U.S. Navy." I responded, "Sir, don't be playing with me, are you serious?" He replied (as if startled), "I am your CO, would I joke about something like that?" I sheepishly apologized because I couldn't believe my ears. I was excited and shocked at the same time. Not knowing whether to laugh or cry, I put a smile on my face.

I then went quietly to the bathroom, got on my knees and said, "Yes, Lord, I'll follow you." On November 29th I received a letter from AFCOE stating my acceptance into their training program. God was making a big point and I definitely took notice. I sent a message to my command thanking everyone for their support but cited Psalm 75:6, 7 as the reason for my promotion. I told them my decision still stood for separation next year, April 29, 2005.

My cohorts still couldn't understand why I would leave the Navy especially now that I was promoted. (*Again, spiritual things are spiritually discerned.*) After all, I was moving up in rank quickly; I would make more money now and be given greater leadership and responsibilities. That knowledge was apparent to me but I knew something that they didn't. I was going to train to rescue men from the greatest battle being fought — the battle of good and evil. I was enlisting into the Lord's army as an active duty soul winner (Proverbs 11:30; Daniel 12:3).

msn♥ Hotmail®

From: Mary Lou Warner marylouw@amazingfacts.org
Sent: Monday, December 6, 2004 4:55 PM
To: "R. C." svg_23@hotmail.com
Subject: RE: AFCOE

MIME-Version: 1.0
Received: from mail.amazingfacts.org ([65.213.198.243]) by mc9-f36.
hotmail.com with Microsoft SMTPSVC(5.0.2195.6824); Mon, 6 Dec
2004 08:56:15 -0800
X-Message-Info: JGTYoYF78jHx/gSwc1Xz9D8kGqR+RIYM
Content-class: urn:content-classes:message
X-MimeOLE: Produced By Microsoft Exchange V6.5.7226.0
X-MS-Has-Attach:
X-MS-TNEF-Correlator:
Thread-Topic: AFCOE
Thread-Index: AcTZbn8+H3tqhAmGQXGP5XvNzuQ5SACRbywA
Return-Path: marylouw@amazingfacts.org
X-OriginalArrivalTime: 06 Dec 2004 16:56:16.0761 (UTC)
FILETIME=[80605690:01C4DBB4]

Dear RC
The committee has met and I sent you an acceptance letter on
November 29. I trust you have received it. Have a blessed day.

Mary Lou Warner

AFCOE Registrar
916-434-3880 ext. 3049

Chapter 13

The Marriage

God is sometimes humorous in His dealings with mankind. He blesses us more than we can imagine. Just saving me would have been enough but as an added gift, He gave me an awesome Christian wife to top it all off. When I first came into the church through water baptism, the last thing on my mind was dating. I just wanted to serve God and was too excited for anything else. However, no matter how hard I fought it, Rhonitta still caught my eyes.

We both were connecting visually for weeks as I tried not to show interest but that didn't last too long. Soon, we became good friends and spent hours on the phone talking about everything. Our friendship grew steadily and on New Year's Day, in 2003, we decided to start a serious dating relationship. Most of our conversations were about life issues and how we wanted to make things better than what we were accustomed to. We wanted to be role models for other young people to emulate.

Rhonitta lived with her mom but her dad was not in the picture. The link that drew us closer was the stroke her mom suffered that put her into a coma not long after we had started dating. It was a pristine sunny Saturday morning in January that Rhona, her mother, came to church and began her regular duties as a deaconess. I had just pulled up in my car, only to be welcomed with the sad report that Rhona said she was feeling hot and then just collapsed. She was rushed immediately to the emergency room at Pavia Hospital in Santurce, Puerto Rico.

The next three weeks were the hardest in Rhonitta's life. Her families came together like never before to support and comfort each other. The church family also rallied around them with love, prayers, and encouragements. When I got off work, I also went to the hospital to visit, sing, pray, and to lend support in any way I could. I was also able to meet other members of the family.

One evening after visitation, I just took a long pause, looked at Rhonitta and felt this heavy impression, "She is the one for you." It was a very strong conviction. "She is the one you will marry." I kept the matter to myself for quite sometime and was especially reluctant to share it during these disturbing times.

The family had so much to deal with and everything intensified when the doctors gave them the tough choice of taking her off life-support. That was a hard call to make on their part and they struggled immensely to come to a unanimous decision. About two weeks later, they returned to the hospital for visitation, hoping they had made the right decision but they did not have to notify the doctors because Rhona had died before their arrival.

It was a terrible loss for all associated with Rhona and the family grieved much. However, they all knew that their mother lived her life for Jesus and were confident that she will rise with the saints when Jesus returns to earth to take us to heaven (1 Thessalonians 4:15-18). Rhona's life bore testimony of her devotion and service for God. Her employers attested to her godly lifestyle, notwithstanding that most of them didn't have a relationship with Christ.

Rhonitta and I continued dating but went slowly as she and her family worked through the grieving process. Meanwhile I was learning all I could about marriage. I read many books and listened to hours of audio programs and radio programs dealing with family life. With all the interesting things I was learning I proceeded to test whether Rhonitta was really the one for me.

I formulated a list of things I must have in a wife and things I wanted but was willing to compromise on. Then I tried her based on these qualifications. I got to see her in many different situations. We had three official break-ups, many disagreements, and extended times apart (including two semesters away for college) all of which stood the test. These served as confirmation for marriage for me but there were still times when I would say yes and other times think it was not the right time. I spoke to her family and dropped subtle hints here and there about one year before I actually proposed.

My pastor and family also gave some wise counsel that helped me to make the big decision. While my dad was on vacation in the Caribbean, he came through Puerto Rico and got a chance to meet her and gave his full approval. My mom spoke with Rhonitta on the phone and knew she was a good woman to marry and that sealed my decision. The guys at the office also gave lots of caution, mainly because they had experienced divorce in the past. I respected their suggestions because I understood where they were coming from, so I took them kindly. I had seen many divorces during my seven years of Naval service both in the military and civilian world but it only strengthened my resolve to set the example. Our relationship was different. We brought biblical principles into the courtship.

Once we started talking about marriage, we were both filled with joy and optimism about the future. The difficult part was deciding on an appropriate date. I wanted to tie the knot before I left the Navy to give us a smooth transition since the end of my obligated service was drawing closer. After about one and a half years of courting, we were engaged August 1, 2004. This was a special occasion and one of the most precious moments in our relationship.

The weekend I decided to propose, I did all I could to get on her nerves and made her upset with me because I knew what I was getting ready to do. That Sunday, I told her to get dressed because I wanted to take her out for lunch at our second favorite hotel in Puerto Rico, The Normandy. When she got ready to go, I purposely did not show up on time. Needless to say she was heated and did not think I was being nice. So I called her again and told her to get dressed (again) and that I would be sending a limousine to pick her up shortly. She did not really believe me but I did show up about two hours later in a plush white Limo with the seats laden with roses and little notes.

I hid in the front seat with the driver so she had no clue I was in the car. I had informed the driver to take us to our favorite place on the island, The Ritz Carlton Hotel. On the way, I would have him pass notes back to her, giving subtle hints of what was taking place. By the time he pulled up to our spot, she had some idea of what was about to happen. I also told the driver to tell her to go to our place because, "Someone is waiting for you back there." After about two minutes, I followed her and by the time I reached her I could see the tears flowing down her gentle cheeks.

The evening was beautiful and the garden area nicely lit. I got on my knees and asked her to begin this journey with me by joining hands in holy matrimony. Through all the tears she managed to say, *"YES."* We then hugged for what seemed an eternity, then knelt down, prayed, and thanked God for this union and asked Him to bless us on this new adventure.

The plan was to marry that Christmas but because we had to be separated a few months, we decided to postpone the wedding until the following June. We did however put together the invitations to begin mailing as soon as possible. My good friend, Carmelo Vega from the U.S. Air Force recruiting office, suggested a unique idea that we'd never heard of before -- DVD invitations. I had no problem having Carmelo handle this project because I trusted him as a fellow military comrade and he had experience with photography and video production, having worked on many wedding projects before. He gave us many wonderful ideas and was pumped as we were to make it happen. In addition, he gave us a huge discount package for both the invitations and wedding recordings.

We were wed the following June and made our home in Huntsville, Alabama, minutes away from the U.S. Space and Rocket Center, Red Stone Arsenal, and Oakwood University. God has equipped me with the perfect help-meet (Genesis 2:24-25; Proverbs 18:22) and and we have decided to do ministry for the Master, using all the resources He has blessed us with.

One thing we had settled before our marriage was the decision to go to AFCOE. We talked about it at great length and we both agreed that it would be better to make the sacrifice early rather than later in our marriage. Knowing God had called us for this purpose, we chose not to put our own personal conveniences ahead of God's calling to go into ministry -- beginning with training at AFCOE.

Many people made this a problem for them but to us it was not a problem at all. There was no compromising on the Commission. Since military spouses could stand by their husbands while taking care of the country's duty, how much more important is it for ministers' wives to stand by their husbands resolutely as they perform the duties of the King of

Kings! Because of this willingness on both our parts, I have grown much closer to my wife and appreciate her in deeper ways than ever before.

Marriage brought much peace to our lives. I no longer try to keep up with the Joneses and waste money here and there in the name of "having a good time." God has given me an exceptional bride who is more than enough for me. One who loves me and complements my God given qualities. He knew what He was doing and put a godly wife in the salvation and ministry package. He blessed me with my own Beautiful Marvelous Wife (BMW).

Rhonitta fulfilled my first and top requirement (priority) in a spouse since she grew up close to the church and was baptized at an early age. This makes a tremendous difference because she is grounded in the Christian faith and that helps to keep our marriage foundation strong. In retrospect (not prophetically), when I first came to Puerto Rico my coworkers told me that single people who come to this island will leave it married and it was interesting to see that fulfilled. Puerto Rico has been a blessing to me and will always have a special place in my heart as the beautiful "isla del encanto."

Chapter 14

The Preparation for Service

Having heard the words, "Whom shall I send, and who will go for us?" my heart ignited to answer the call, "Here I am, send me." (Isaiah 6:8) Just like the Navy, I needed a boot camp type of training and AFCOE had the right caliber. Since they train committed and consecrated saints to become frontline soldiers on the battlefield of the great controversy, God led me here to be under their tutelage to prepare for His service. The military's training is not only theoretical but more practical and hands-on -- this attracted me to AFCOE's method! I also needed something dynamic, intense and effective while learning all aspects of evangelism like: public and personal outreach programs, preaching, church planting and Biblical counseling. Since becoming a Christian, I am very careful to continually educate myself in the ways of Jesus Christ and the courses offered suited my style of learning.

The caption that really solidified my choice was in their handbook, "Students do not just learn about their faith — they live and share it." How could I not get excited about that? Furthermore, AFCOE promised that students will discover the Bible and the Lord like never before and to expect enthusiastic, skilled instructors with years of experience in practical and effective evangelism. It goes on:

> "At AFCOE, students would: develop
> confidence and skills to witness and
> teach any time or place, master frequently
> misunderstood Bible doctrines, get hands-
> on experience during a live crusade and
> learn to conduct powerful and convincing
> Bible studies and evangelistic seminars.
> An important part of the training is the
> practical applications of the knowledge
> students learn in class. Instructions include
> regular opportunities for students to develop

their skills and gifts in real-life experiences
with non-believers and work in teams of
two under the supervision and guidance
of experienced Bible workers, pastors, and
evangelists. They seek to take non-believers
from the point of initial contact all the way
through to baptism and full profession of
faith.

Participation in a local evangelistic
crusade conducted by Amazing Facts and
AFCOE also provide an important part of
the training. Interested graduates will have
the opportunity to present an evangelistic
series of their own, both locally and interna-
tionally. Some ministries in which students
will participate may include: prayer ministries, friendship evangelism, finding and
getting people to study the Bible, visiting
people who have responded to Amazing
Facts media programs, reclaiming former
and missing members, sharing video and
audiotapes, running a correspondence
Bible school, leading small-group studies,
evangelistic visitation, gaining decisions,
preparing people for baptism, and

disciplining of new believers. With the unique design of these classes, each student will get the personal attention they need to develop their soul-winning potential." (*Amazing Facts College of Evangelism Handbook, p.14* [paraphrased]).

That was exactly what I needed to hear and God had sent me the tools to be effective in ministering to people.

Chapter 15

The Saint and the Ministry

y friend, this is an exciting time to be alive and especially now that I have discovered my purpose for living. As world events foreshadow our Lord's iminent return, people are sleeping while their destinies are hanging in the balance. Sin has desensitized our world and Satan has convinced the majority that he does not exist. Many are living today anyway they want and have no desire for spiritual things. I am appalled that we live in a "free society" yet are enslaved by all this godlessness!

We have so much wealth but are losing our health. We have so many churches yet moral degeneracy is rampant. The Commandments of God are lightly regarded by both Christians and secular America. God commissions us to spread His Words to a spiritually bankrupt nation and world and that is exactly what I have surrendered the rest of my life to do. In Proverbs 11:30 the famous king Solomon recognized that *winning souls* for God is *wise.*

Why should we only reach for worldly acclaim when our brothers, friends, families, shipmates, and nation miss out on the most important decisions of their lives? In this lifetime of ours, there are only two choices that matter. There are no fences and no middle grounds. When all is said and done, we are either God's or Satan's, lost or saved, good or evil. We will either spend eternity in heaven or be eternally separated from God. People seem to think that if they just live decent lives that will suffice but the only surety of eternal life with Jesus Christ is knowing Him as Lord and Personal Savior. That is exactly what we want to help people to do. I don't know what your circumstances are but aren't you tired of living a life of dissatisfaction? Tired of playing games? Tired of trying to live up to the status quo? Aren't you just plain tired of being tired? I simply desire to help people see that there is more to life than meets the eyes and everything that glitters is not gold.

There is much work to be done but together we can make a unified effort to stand for this bastion of truth — the everlasting gospel. I cannot and will not deny the power of God to save and the deliverance I found by a saving relationship with Jesus Christ. The Bible admonishes, *"How beautiful on the mountains are the feet of those who bring good news, who proclaim peace, who bring good tidings, who proclaim salvation, who say to Zion, 'Your God reigns!'"* (Isaiah 52:7) It also declares in Romans 10:14-16, *"How, then, can they call on the one they have not believed in? And how can they believe in the one of whom they have not heard? And how can they hear without someone preaching to them? And how can they preach unless they are sent? As it is written, 'How beautiful are the feet of those who bring good news.'"*

It is my Christian duty to warn men and women about the deceptions which ensnare our souls and point them to the solution to the world's greatest need. Let us sound that certain trumpet to those who will listen and even to those who might reject because I want people to be delivered like I was a few years ago. While freedom still rings, God says, *"You must speak my words to them, whether they listen or fail to listen, for they are rebellious."* (Ezekiel 2:7)

My friend, God has called me to share the good news of salvation and His love for all people. With Jesus there is freedom. The Bible plainly says that, *"if the Son (of God) sets you free, you are free indeed,"* (John 8:36) and His purpose is to set captives free and proclaim liberty to all who will accept Him and His words as Truth (Isaiah 61:1,2). I'm compelled to teach people everywhere how to find liberty from physical, financial, and spiritual bondage through testimonies, seminars, literature, missionary work, and other sources. To borrow a quote from one of my favorite authors, we are "lesser lights pointing to the Greater Light."

Rhonitta and I are prepared to walk this journey and we want you to stand with us so we can do it together. Become a part of this important work today. If the Lord is leading your heart, then do not hesitate to respond. Please share this book with others and get a copy for everyone you know. Send especially a copy to our military men and women both at home and abroad.

We can all learn from each other to help others avoid some pitfalls in life. I've learned some of life's greatest lessons from the lives of mentors. Share your copy of this book if you must and send us an email or letter of your testimony on how this message has touched your life. I'm also available to share this and many empowering principles at your church, home, military chapel, family reunion, or school.

Rhonitta and I are currently serving as missionaries with the National Association for the Prevention of Starvation (NAPS), a multifaceted, mission-driven, youth organization bringing physical and spiritual relief to thousands in the U.S. and around the world.

We have ministered to some of the most at-risk and neglected people in: Decatur and Kilpatrick, AL; Lake Charles, LA; Dallas and Houston, TX; New York, NY; Camden, NJ; Miami, FL; Chicago, IL; Radcliff, KY; Indianapolis, IN; Silver Spring, MD; Boston, MA; Chesapeake and Virginia Beach, VA; and Atlanta, GA. We've also been privileged to be a part of laboring for over 3,000 souls baptized into the body of Christ and almost 1,000 youth trained in evangelism in the US and overseas in: Zimbabwe, Madagascar, Botswana, Mozambique, Zambia, and Liberia.

I'll be sharing more on our ministry with NAPS in a subsequent book. I couldn't include my exciting adventures on numerous NAPS missions in this book because it would have been too long. So stay tuned for that edition. Please pray for us and support our mission agency—NAPS. Review this humble ministry online and give your donations at *www. napsoc.org* or call 256-726-7056.

You can also volunteer your time and energies with other outreach agencies like NAPS that are spreading the gospel message. Get involved today. Sow a seed and watch God give an abundant harvest. Thank you very much for your time, prayers, and efforts in advance. *"Finally, be strong in the Lord and in his mighty power."* (Ephesians 6:10)

Chapter 16

The AFCOE Experience

This chapter was added after the book was written because I really felt I must share a little about what God taught me while at AFCOE. It would be impossible to tell you in full details all the wonderful blessings and lessons this training taught me. From the very first day I arrived until graduation, the learning never ceased.

Upon arrival at the college it was a pleasure finally getting to meet the staff of this dynamic ministry and putting faces to the voices I used to hear on the phone. Upon check-in I also began meeting the various students from different countries and states. Since I thrive in diversity, I was happy to see students from as far as South Africa and Australia and still nearer, Canada and Florida. The ages ranged from eighteen to sixty-six, married and singles alike. It was an awesome combination of people and to think that we were all destined to be here for this appointed time was a humbling experience for all.

My expectations were surpassed by the depth and wealth of knowledge received. From day one we were getting solid meat and learned some revolutionary methods for evangelism. Everything was so applicable that even if I had left the training halfway through the course, I would be very capable of doing much good and launching a ministry. The students were model Christians themselves because everyone abandoned the security of their comfort zones. People left jobs, families, homes, endured separation and so much more, in order to pursue God's calling on their lives. It was a tough challenge to trust and depend upon God for absolutely everything and especially finances. It was at AFCOE that I had decidedly surrendered my total financial dependence upon God and to do things His way.

"Seek ye first the kingdom of God and His righteousness and these things shall be added on to you" (Matthew 5:33) became very real and personal to me. Likewise,

I claimed the promise of Luke 10:38 as my own, *"No man having left father and mother and wife and lands and children shall not be rewarded one hundred fold in this life with persecution and in the one to come, eternal life."*

Sharing a room in a college-like setting was not something I was particularly thrilled about but in this Christian environment, I could not have asked for better roommates. They were the perfect match. These two men of God were very humble and they contributed to a pleasant AFCOE experience. John was Chinese while Curtis was half Korean. What a mix! While John, the younger, was more easy-going and laid back, Curtis was very studious and disciplined. His daily devotional life and fitness regimen were an example for both of us.

The church we worked with for the evangelistic series helped the students in many ways. Not only did we contribute to a successful meeting but the members themselves displayed the best hospitality I had ever experienced at any church. They prayed for the students, made their homes available for rest and play and also helped counsel several students. I had never seen a body of believers come together like that before and it made me all the more appreciative that we had this practicum. The series culminated with a baptism ceremony of forty plus saints. It was indeed an abundant blessing for weeks of hard work.

I learned valuable lessons in the classroom but the lessons I learned outside the classroom were more precious. Behind the scenes I was being tried and tested in my faith and dedication to the Lord. While transformed into a disciple no doubt, I still had much work to undergo in character building. The hardest thing for me was to trust God unconditionally in the area of finances. It was a constant struggle for me and much prayer. Though I was not alone, I feared seeing the brook of financial provision dry up. My faith was severely tried as I watched my savings and investments slowly dwindle. I had to pray tirelessly for strength and courage to trust God. Holding on to my credit card as a reserve, I was challenged to rely on God only and learn to walk by faith.

One afternoon as I was resting in bed, I felt such a peace that was reassuring. I knelt and gave God full responsibility for provisions and He never failed me yet. Throughout my training I never lacked anything I needed. Even when I completely ran out of money, God provided in many surprising ways. He used students, staff, church members, and divine appointments to meet every need at hand. Now I can look back and see why I needed to go through that experience as it has proven to be helpful in my ministry to others.

Another area of my life that needed attention was my level of commitment to this work. In my heart and soul I knew I wanted to follow Jesus and had calculated the cost of discipleship. However, I still had not given my heart unreservedly over to the Lord for ministry only. Somehow I was still hoping to leave a back door open just in case and had many secular ideas for making a living that needed to be dealt with. God was calling me to be His man and to be sold out to His Gospel Commission. Coming home from the nightly meetings stirred within me an even greater need to really share the gospel.

These truths of scripture are what people need and I must tell it to everyone. As I sat through the series and listened to the man of God present the messages in such a clear, convincing, and convicting manner, I felt stirred and sad at the same time. Stirred because the words were like fire in my bones and sad because I knew my family needed to hear these profound truths of the Bible. "Oh how I wished they were there listening, there was no doubt they would be converted!"

It is said that the hardest people to reach and witness to are your own family members and there is much truth to that statement. However, I made up my mind that I would take these same messages to my family when I graduated. The Lord laid it on my heart to seek His face and I prayed to Him and surrendered the rest of my life to reach the lost in whatever capacity He saw fit. I enlisted in His service full time and decided that I would go all the way for my Savior.

Chapter 17

The Evolution of a Book

The third thing I want to share with you is the best thing that happened to me at AFCOE. You would not be reading this book had I not gone to AFCOE. The providential leadings for writing this book are amazing. I smile every time I think about them.

As you know, I had already written fourteen pages of my personal testimony which I shared at the youth event in Homestead, Florida, in October, 2004. But I never planned on finishing it anytime soon. It was a project I had put on my goals list for a future date because I was gathering research information for another book I was working on and was anxious to publish. I even took the outline and the notes for that book I had already gathered to AFCOE and as time permitted, I worked on it. That soon changed, however, and that's why you're reading this book first.

Preaching for decisions was one of our classes and one assignment was to share our personal testimony. I didn't take it too seriously and gave a brief spiel to the class when it came my turn to share. An interesting event occurred almost a month before graduation. A pastor from Texas was coming to the college to interview candidates for a position at his church so our outreach coordinator called me into her office to ask me if I was interested. As we spoke, she asked me how long I'd been a Christian and I shared with her how I came to learn the truth. She was touched by what I shared and asked me if I would be willing to share my testimony in two weeks with the staff at their morning devotions. And of course, I agreed.

Three days earlier, I was reading the book *My Two Witnesses* and it challenged believers to share their testimony and witness to others. It was a simple message but the way it was presented brought a stern rebuke and conviction in my heart. Any and everyone can share their personal testimony!

The morning I shared my testimony at the Amazing Facts staff devotion, a series of events were triggered that produced this work in your hands today. After devotions, three people approached me about doing an article of some sort and had a good caption for the sailor turned saint. They asked me to put together something for them to put in print. I went to Mrs. Carolyn Moxley, the Bible school superintendent, to get the exact dates that I started and finished the Bible study guides. Mrs. Moxley had the biggest smile I'd seen in months because she was so pleased to hear me share my testimony and to finally meet one of her baptized students. She had no idea I was attending the AFCOE program and told me she had shared my story at a similar meeting and showed me the notes she had kept on record.

I always wanted to meet her because I only communicated with her through letters. She was also the one who sent me the addresses for churches in Puerto Rico.

Next, I was scheduled to share a brief five-minute testimony on live television at Sacramento Central Church which really got my attention that maybe I really had something worth telling. This was a nerve-racking experience but thanks to my witty instructor, I made it through. Things were falling into place without my consent.

By this time, AFCOE was in full swing with an evangelistic series and I saw God transform lives night by night. On the way home one evening about halfway through the meetings, it happened. While John and the other students conversed about the nightly subjects, I sat in the back seat of his car, buried in thoughts about life in general. Then it struck me like a lightning bolt: *From Sailor to Saint!* "Write a book on your personal testimony and call it *From Sailor to Saint*." The entire outline was vividly stamped in my mind and I chewed on it the remainder of the way home. As soon as I got to my room, I jotted down the title and chapters on a piece of paper and called my friend James about the revelation. I shared with him what had been going on and what just happened and he was excited and thought it sounded good.

When we hung up I called my wife and told her and she liked it too but I still didn't make any plans to write a book just yet. Thanksgiving was drawing near and I was looking forward to seeing my wife (though we went back and forth about the certainty of her flying to California).

One Saturday afternoon after church, I stayed behind in the prayer room so I could do some Bible studies. While looking for reading material, I chanced upon a book the youth pastor was reading. The title was fascinating so I picked it up and began browsing through the table of contents. I noticed a chapter about giving your personal testimony and thought to myself, "Now that's weird." I read the chapter, took some notes and couldn't help but meditate on what all this meant.

It was then I reasoned with myself, "Why not write this book first? I don't need any extensive research because it's my own life and I already have fourteen pages." Pure joy welled up inside and I called Rhonitta to tell her about it. We both were sounding like kids again. Since our schedules conflicted for Thanksgiving and we couldn't maximize the time-off, we decided it was best to just finish the book over the break and wait two more weeks until we saw each other again.

I didn't have a computer at AFCOE so I asked one of the students, a good friend, to loan me her laptop for the five days of Thanksgiving break so I could finish writing the book. I was so happy she said yes and stayed up until early mornings writing away. Sometimes I went to bed at daybreak because the hours just seemed to fly by and I paid no notice of it. I took a little break on Thanksgiving Day for dinner but went right back to writing afterwards. When we returned to class after the break, I had a manuscript to work with and had brought a dream to life! All I did for the remainder of the program was edit here and there, adding any pertinent details I remembered. When I looked at all the pages I had in my hand, my heart was both satisfied and humbled.

My dear reader, I cannot begin to tell you how much it means to me that you are reading this book. This may be the only way I could ever communicate with you and that to me is a huge blessing. It's no small thing that you are reading my story, surely it was meant to be.

Some people will call this kind of thing luck, destiny, or coincidence, but call it what you may, I call it a divine appointment made by God. I pray that you'll be blessed, challenged, and transformed as a result. All of our lives are precious and we can certainly learn from each other. Let this final chapter speak to your heart and soul as you contemplate the message it was meant to convey. God be with you.

Chapter 18

The Appeal

My precious friend, I wrote this book out of a deep desire to let my comrades understand a mystery about the lives we live. Please, give it some deep thought because even the biggest skeptic can stand to gain something new. If you will at least meditate upon these words then a victory has been won. Lend these few pages your undivided attention because much is at stake.

True peace and contentment can never be found in anything or anyone except a lasting relationship with Jesus Christ. The value of your life is not measured by the abundance of things you own. What good is it if you have everything the world could offer and all your heart's desires yet lose your soul? How much are you worth? What will you give in exchange for your soul? (See Luke 12:15 and Mark 8:34-38) Look closely at the life you're living and you will discover that whatever captivates you, that is what you're willing to lose your soul for. That is what you're worth!

Take these questions very seriously. My goal is not to chastise, judge or condemn in any way. This comes from a sincere heart of love that is burdened for you and I take the precious time to write and warn you about the landmines that are before you. Please consider this appeal as a shipmate looking out for another shipmate. After all, that is what military personnel do. We take care of each other. In the same way, we are in a real spiritual warfare and it is my duty to inform the troops about the dangers on this mission.

When was the last time you earnestly spent some good quality time with yourself? Quality time to decipher where your life is heading or what really matters the most to you? Only you know yourself and only you can answer for the life you truly desire and the things that weigh heavily on your heart. Many things have happened in my own life that brought me to a place where I had to spend that quality time all by myself and answer these same questions.

Even if you need to take some leave and get away by yourself, do it now! Don't let your life be driven by the snares of Satan. Too many people live without any real thought about why they do what they do. You have a choice, so choose wisely the life you want to live. Stop permitting circumstances to dictate your life and measuring yourself by society's lanyard. Where have you been? Where are you going? What do you want to be when you get there? Who is going with you? How does the future look from where you are today? Are you satisfied with that?

Put on your thinking caps and follow me along this path. Have you ever wondered, "Why is our society so spiritually bankrupt? Why are immorality (and all the sexual connotations that go with that word) and financial bondage (in the form of excessive credit, debts, loans, and bankruptcy) so prevalent today?"

With a little research, you'll be startled by the alarming statistics. You'll realize the distressing fact that the two leading causes for our young people and adults alike running from God and turning to secularism are moral decadence (and all that this stands for) and the love of money (greediness). Let that one penetrate your mind for a while. Everyone may not be in this predicament but it's the case for the vast majority of Americans. Just examine the trends and the statistics will startle you.

Knowing that there is a right and better way to live, why continue to sell yourself as a slave to immorality and financial bondage? Many are living a fake life. A lifestyle bought on credit (literally speaking). The popular thing is that everyone owes somebody or something and lives from paycheck-to-paycheck. The quote "I owe, I owe, so off to work I go" is the unfortunate reality for the masses.

People are constantly living in fear because if they lose their jobs today or tomorrow, there goes the car, there goes the fine clothes, and there goes the popularity. Then, here comes disappointment, disaster, and depression. Revelation 3:14-22 rightfully describes these times we live in and I urge you to read these verses because the message demands close investigation.

Don't take the hard route. Learn from the errors of others. I had taken many things for granted and was just "going with the flow" (like many of you are right now). Will it take adversity or tragedy to force you to change? It doesn't have to be that way. Take counsel and be wise.

Are you chasing after the wind? I had been pursuing a fantasy life like many of you but if you should heed this appeal, you can certainly avoid the landmines ahead. Take it from me please, "You're headed for destruction and a whole lot of heartaches." At this point you may be wondering, "How do I avoid these pitfalls?" Good question. Let me tell you how I was rescued.

The Lord Jesus Christ came to this earth on a rescue operation some two thousand years ago for mankind. The reconnaissance was determined long before you and I came into the picture. Satan is the archrival, and his plot is to destroy all life. He is a liar and a deceiver and his decoys serve the purpose of keeping us eternally separated from a loving God. In order for us to be restored in the image of God, Jesus had to suffer and die on Calvary's cross (Romans 5:8-11). This was His sacrifice for mankind, not because we deserved it but because He loves us so much. It is a FREE gift that's offered for all people — no strings attached (John 3:16, 17).

Military men and women put their lives on the line everyday so that the rest of us can live in peace. Their service is at least compensated for but Jesus did not charge anything to our account. He was willing to pay the death penalty so we can enjoy true freedom and peace from the world's delusions. We cannot overcome our sinful condition. It takes a saving relationship with God to overcome sin.

This gift is freely offered to you today. It remains free until you take it. You only need accept Jesus' sacrifice and forgiveness then you can turn around and start living with hope. Contentment and righteous living can only be obtained by living in harmony with the Biblical principles of Jesus Christ. You must have a relationship with Him. Will you make that decision today? It's the most significant decision you'll ever make in this life. Do it now!

Please take this caution very seriously, my friend. This is not about trying to be a good person or living a decent life. If you think that's what this is all about, then you've missed the big picture. I want you to understand and realize that you have to get back to what really matters; get back to God, get back in touch with the Bible, be a part of the church again, and live righteously before a Holy and Just God. Jesus is still a forgiving God, just waiting for you to accept His loving advances. Don't forget He lets you breathe that breath you just took, and that one too, and the next one you're about to take.

There's no depth of sin and pain where God cannot reach you. In fact, I know He's talking to you right now and still pleading with you to come home to Him. Isn't it time you did?

God has not left His place but we are the ones who choose to leave His side. All the partying and material possessions cannot settle what you truly long for. Don't think like many people who feel they will just have fun now and then later start living a righteous life. That's an illusion, my friend, and a dangerous presumption. Make the changes today. Start turning your heart to Jesus now, only He can give you unconditional love and genuine forgiveness.

Like a brother to a brother (or sister), I'm speaking with a heavy heart for my people, especially the youth. It shocks me to see that many are running from the doors of church or anything that has to do with the name of God or Jesus. It's not just a problem in these United States of America but a universal problem.

We're engaged in a spiritual warfare, whether you want to realize it or not. The devil seeks to hold you a slave to sin by feeding you a counterfeit lifestyle. I am here to proclaim to you that Satan cannot keep you in shackles because his fate is already sealed. You can choose your destiny today by exercising your God-given freedom of choice. I'm urging you out of love and appreciation, choose life!

Take some time for yourself and contemplate what matters most in your life. Will the academic degrees make you content? A PhD does not give you theological correctness and that new business venture may not bring you your desired success, for these too shall perish. Will the new Mercedes Benz finally give you inner peace? Its value depreciates the moment you drive off the lot. Will landing that six figure income job and a fat bank account give you the security you covet? Heaven and eternity are free and being there is priceless.

Please, be honest with yourself and do what needs to be done. Make time and room for Jesus Christ. Why not give this new life a try? Haven't you tried everything else and realized they do not satisfy? Turn now to the King of the universe and experience the difference only He can make. Even the wise King Solomon in all his glory and riches confessed it was all vanity and chasing after the wind. He finally realized his emptiness and gave us this wisdom key, *"Fear God, and keep His commandments for this is the whole duty of man. For God shall bring every work into judgment, with every secret thing, whether it be good, or whether it be evil."* (Ecclesiastes 12:12-14) God's Commandments are not grievous but He offers love and rest for your weary, thirsty soul (1 John 5:2, 3; Matthew 11:28; Isaiah 55:1-2).

Dear reader, God is waiting to receive you in His Kingdom so accept His loving offer today. Remember, everything that glitters is not gold and there is always more than meets the eyes. Therefore, walk wisely (not in worldly wisdom) as you make the most of your time on this earth because the times in which we live are getting worse (Ephesians 5:15-17; Ecclesiastes 12:1).

> *"So I tell you this, and insist on it in the Lord, that you must no longer live as the Gentiles do, in the futility of their thinking. They are darkened in their understanding and separated from the life of God because of the ignorance that is in them due to the hardening of their hearts. Having lost all sensitivity, they have given themselves over to sensuality so as to indulge in every kind of impurity, with a continual lust for more." You, however, did not come to know Christ that way. Sure you heard of Him and were taught in Him in accordance with the Truth that is in Jesus. You were taught, with regard to your former way of life, to put off your old self, which is being corrupted by its deceitful desires, to be made new in the attitude of your minds, and to put on the New Self, created to be like God in true righteousness and holiness.* (Ephesians 4:17-24 NIV --emphasis mine)

Jesus is tenderly pleading with you saying, *"Take my yoke upon you, and learn of me; for I am meek and lowly in heart: and ye shall find rest unto your souls. For my yoke is easy, and my burden is light."* (Matthew 11:29-30) It's just that simple, my friend. In fact, it's so simple, most people make it hard.

Christ died for all mankind because we are all sinful. He did not come to call those who are already Christians but for people who may not even know they need Jesus. He came to give us new life and purpose. The promise is given, *"if we confess our sins, He is faithful and just to forgive us our sins and to cleanse us from all unrighteousness."* (1 John 1:9) Follow that simple step to begin a new life today and remember, *"he that covers his sins shall not prosper, but he who confesses and forsakes his sins shall have mercy."* (Proverbs 28:13 NKJV) Can you find any greater love than this? Is that wonderful news or what? It sure was good news for me. God is an awesome God!

I'm so glad I don't need to chase after the fake stuff any more nor waste my substance trying to impress others. Thanks be to God who gave me the victory and intervened in my life on that December day in 1999 aboard the U.S.S. Frank Cable. He took time just for me and He is taking time just for you too.

Society may make you feel that all you need in this life is a six-figure job with a nice office overlooking the ocean, the mansion on the hill with your high school sweetheart, the perfect set of children, and that will make you happy and content. Well, by now you are aware that the American dream comes with a big price tag. A price tag that has eternal consequences and has plunged many into slavery.

The media is not "reality TV." The music stars sing the most bizarre songs and movies portray misconceptions about love and marriage. How can we base our success on what the media portrays? How can we make idols out of stars who call women derogatory names and use profanity in every verse of their songs and on the TV screens? Something is seriously wrong with this picture!

Read these words very carefully. Give them your complete attention. God has placed before you life and death today. Choose life and live! I can honestly say, *"I have not yet attained nor arrived at perfection but this one thing I do; forgetting those things in the past and reaching forth by faith to the life God has set before me."* (Philippians 3:12-14 -- emphasis mine)

By God's grace and infinite mercy, I will one day receive all the glories of heaven, which makes the temporary pleasures of this world pale in comparison. It's not by our efforts that we'll get into heaven nor is it the luxury cars or the people of influence we know (Ephesians 2:8-10). No, my friend. All that matters would be to hear Jesus our Savior say, *"Enter into the joy of thy Lord."* (Matthew 25:21, 23) What better words can you hear? Incredible!

Take advantage of this opportunity now. Freedom still reigns in our world today, but true freedom can only be won when Jesus Christ reigns supreme on the throne of your heart. What do you say to that? You've tried everything the world says will bring satisfaction. Are you satisfied and happy?

I've been where you are headed and done most of what you want to do. It still leaves you empty. Jesus is the solution. He really saves. He saw through my inadequacy and filled the void in my heart. Now I can say with contentment, "I am transformed from sailor to saint." You too can be changed from who you are today to what God originally intended. Give Him a chance to transform you and I guarantee one thousand percent, you will not be disappointed! Accept Jesus as your Lord and Savior today (John 3:16). Do it now!

Is There Any Greater Love?

Copyright © by Kolongi.com (used by permission)

Appendix & Resources

Meridian, MS

ESWS Pin qualification (L-R):
SK3 (SW) Chance (me); SK3 (SW) Pahati

Newly promoted sailors (L-R):
SK1 Mancilla, SK2 (SW) Chance (me),
SK1 (SW) Martir, SK2 (SW) Hollis.

Rented BMW on NAS1
Base in Sigonella, Sicily

On the way to Palermo
(Sicily) with friends.

My first car - Nissan Maxima
in Aguana, Guam

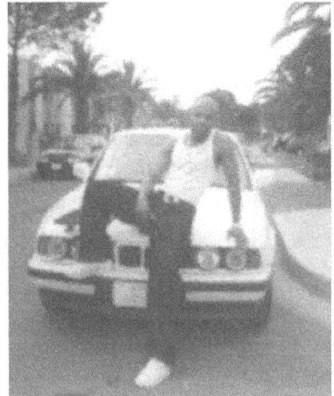

My second car - BMW
520I in Sicily, Italy

Rented Mercedes Benz

"All that glitters is not gold"

Return visit to Guam

My BMW – Beautiful Marvelous Wife

Puerto Rico - La isla del
encanta

Yokosuka, Japan

Baptism Ceremony

Amazing Facts Center of Evangelism, Winter 2005

Pastor Doug Batchelor

P.O. Box 1058 • Roseville, CA 95678-8058 • 916-434-3880 • Fax 916-434-3889 • www.amazingfacts.org

December 2005

It's time to drop everything else! The harvest is ripe!

And as we close this incredible year of sowing gospel seed, I feel like the farmer whom Jesus talked about in Mark 4:26–29. The Bible says he planted a field and watched the seeds sprout and grow. And even though he didn't understand how, the soil produced the grain ...

"But when the fruit is brought forth, immediately he putteth in the sickle, because the harvest is come" (Mark 4:29).

I'll admit that most times, I don't even know all the ways that God is using **Amazing Facts**. But I do know this: The fruitfulness of our work together is paying off in a bumper crop of souls being won to Christ every single day. The harvest is ready. It's time to get to work!

Looking back at the astounding events of 2005, your prayers and gifts to support the proclamation of the gospel through **Amazing Facts** came just in time for millions of souls.

Randrick Chance was one of them. He found an **Amazing Facts** Bible Study Guide in a magazine rack on his Navy ship and was captivated by the practical lessons from the Bible. The seeds of his curiosity quickly sprouted into a passionate pursuit of the gospel truth. Later he completed the Bible study course, was baptized, and started sharing Christ with others in his unit.

Today he is a student at our **Amazing Facts** Center for Evangelism (AFCOE), preparing to proclaim the gospel as an evangelist!

Randrick understands that it's harvest time—he dropped everything, left his promising military career, and "put in his sickle." I love to see young men like him driven with passion for souls. It's contagious!

And I hope it is contagious with you as well for two critical reasons: First, your prayers and financial gifts are helping to change lives like Randrick's all over the world. The seeds of the gospel that you have helped scatter to the farthest corners of the world through **Amazing Facts** are taking root, and producing fruit!

A NEW CHANCE

RANDRICK BECOMES A SOLDIER FOR CHRIST

BY RANDRICK CHANCE

I grew up attending church and even got baptized. But after a few years in the Navy, my philosophy about life radically changed. My idea of success was making lots of money, driving the best cars, and partying every weekend. I found self-worth by dressing in the trendiest clothes, wearing expensive jewelry, and impressing the ladies.

My peers thought I was living the good life. Outwardly, I seemed happy and in control—but within I was miserable and without purpose. Under the mask of success, I was terribly insecure. I wondered how someone like me, who had everything a young person could want, could be so lonely? I was utterly depressed.

U.S.S. PROVIDENCE?

That's when God gave me my first encounter with real biblical substance. While on duty on a naval warship, browsing through a magazine rack looking for something to just kill some time, I discovered an Amazing Facts Study Guide. The title was so startling that I was compelled to pick it up. It turned out to be the beginning of an adventure in discovering God in a completely new way.

I started the lessons with much excitement. I could not wait to get the next one in the mail. Shortly after, I transferred to Italy, and a great controversy began to play out in my life. There were temptations like never before, and I kept falling for the fake life of the world as I struggled to continue the lessons.

Chance found this Study Guide aboard his naval ship.

However, I experienced another breakthrough when I got to the lesson "Lost Day of History." It really opened my eyes. Though still not fully converted, I managed well for a time and found peace, but I still had the same friends and influences. Eventually, I fell back to my old habits.

LASTING RESOLVE

Later, I was transferred to Puerto Rico, and it was there that I really sensed my need for Jesus. Since I was new to Puerto Rico, I didn't have any family or friends there, so I had a lot of time to focus on God and let Him work on my heart. I soaked up each guide's truth like a sponge; soon I was ready to take my stand for Jesus. I contacted Carolyn Moxley, an Amazing Facts representative, about churches in Puerto Rico and she quickly and warmly responded. I then completed the 27 lessons and was baptized!

It has been an awesome journey since I accepted Jesus to rule on the throne of my heart! Praise Him, He had a special calling on my life and has used my passion to let me speak during church services. I even became a youth leader and was invited to preach in Florida for a youth weekend event.

A DIFFERENT KIND OF SOLDIER

Recently, the Lord led me to the Amazing Facts Center of Evangelism. I prayed and fasted, and I felt certain it was part of His will. But honestly, I still had a little doubt, so I asked a specific sign. I told that Lord that if He promoted me one more time in the Navy, I would know He wanted me to go to the School of Evangelism. Incredibly, not long after, I was in fact promoted!

I was excited and shocked at the same time. Beyond a shadow of a doubt, I knew the Lord was telling me to let go of the Navy and follow Him all the way. After being honorably discharged, God led me to an incredible school! It has been the perfect training program for me.

There have been great changes in my life, and God has freed me from many hurtful desires. By the loving mercies and grace of Jesus, I am overcoming the world one step at a time. I have peace knowing I am secure in Christ. God has realigned my priorities so that now I desire to do His will and have totally surrendered to His ministry full-time.

I found out that Jesus, and not the world, is the answer to a spiritually bankrupt world, and He has indeed made a difference in my life. Thank you, Amazing Facts, for being there to help me along the way.

Recommended Resources

I've included the following meaningful highlighted publications, media, and awards for your review. Some links may be inactive due to website updates.

- Amazing Facts December 2005 Ministry Correspondence Letter.

- Inside Report Magazine July/August 2006, page 26 http://www.amazingfacts.org/portals/0/PDFs/NukeNews/File2/july2006.pdf and June 2007.

- Pacific Union Recorder -- Volume 106, issue 2, February 1, 2006. http://www.pacificunionrecorder.com/106/2/

- Southern Tidings -- February 2006, page 19 http://www.southernunion.com/tidingspdf/Feb06Tidings.pdf

- Adventist-Laymen Services and Industries (ASI) April 2007 website article: http://www.asiministries.org/article.php?id=127&PHPSESSID=150b881fa072e96f272a5a92a7ca317a

- South Central Conference of SDA website article 4/10/2007:http://www.scc-adventist.org/news-pressreleases-detail.cfm?id=200

- Navy/Marine Corps Achievement Medal (4), Navy "E" Ribbon (2), Navy Good Conduct Medal (3), National Defense Service Medal (2), Global War on Terrorism Service Medal, Sea Service Deployment Ribbon (2), Navy/Marine Corps Overseas Service Ribbon (6), Navy Recruiting Service Ribbon (5), NATO Medal, Enlisted Surface Warfare Specialist (ESWS) Badge, Sailor of the Quarter (2000 – 2002).

- Sacramento Central SDA Church TV Broadcast aired November 5, 2005.

- 3ABN Television Broadcast (2008; 2009; 2010)

- Important Bible Subjects Revisited, unpublished manuscript, 2009.

- Principles of Successful Christian Living, unpublished manuscript, 2010.

- Amazing Stories of Changed Lives. http://www.amazingfacts.org/DonateOnline/AmazingStories/tabid/256/articleType/ArticleView/articleId/156/ANew-Chance-Randrick-Becomes-a-Soldier-for-Christ.aspx.

- Amazing Facts Center of Evangelism (AFCOE) testimony article, "Soul Mission" http://www.afcoe.org/afcoe-in-action/testimonies/articletype/articleview/articleid/76/soul-mission.aspx.

These excellent books will help you find your purpose and connect with God. Try reading all of them, especially the Bible.

- *The Holy Bible* — KJV, NKJV, NASB, NIV
- *Steps to Christ* — Ellen G. White
- *To See The King* — Doug Batchelor
- *The Certaity of God's Promises* — Randrick Chance
- *Marriage Principles* — Randrick Chance
- *Living the Life of Faith* — Randrick Chance
- *Important Bible Subjects Revisited* — Randrick Chance
- *Principles of Successful Christian Living* — Randrick Chance
- *An Army of Youth* — NAPS
- *To Live in His Sight* — Leslie Kay
- *Escape to God* — Jim Hohnberger
- *Theo-Economics* — Dr. Roland J. Hill
- *The Great Controversy* — Ellen G. White
- *Higher Still* — Wellesley Muir
- *His Robe or Mine* — Frank Phillips
- *Lessons on Faith* — A.T. Jones and E.J. Waggoner
- *Ten Commandments Twice Removed* — Danny Shelton and Shelly J. Quinn
- *The Desire of Ages* — Ellen G. White
- *The Witnessing Church* — Derrick Hall
- *A Knock at Midnight* — Dr. Martin Luther King Jr.
- *Haiti and Haitians* — Simeon S. Nerelus
- *Success God's Way* — Dr. Charles F. Stanley
- *Mission Pilot* — David Gates
- *UnRapped* — Melanie Scherencel Bockmann
- *Revolution in World Missions* – Dr. K.P. Yohannan

Here are some great websites to help you develop in every area of your life. Save or bookmark them so you can continually refer to them.

- www.allpowerseminar.com
- www.bibleuniverse.com
- www.amazingfacts.org
- www.goallpower.com
- www.audioverse.org
- www.gopreach.org
- www.napsoc.org
- www.crown.org
- www.3abn.org
- www.7smr.org
- www.haiti411.com
- www.drpipipm.org
- www.bibleuniverse.com
- www.whitehorsemedia.com
- www.amazingdiscoveries.org
- www.marriageprinciples.com
- www.remnantpublications.com
- extraordinarylifestylesecrets.com
- dailysuccesshabits.com
- strategicsecrets.com

Here are some of the places I've traveled to:
- Australia (Darwin)
- Barbados
- Botswana (Francistown, Tutume)
- China (Hong Kong)
- Guam
- Italy
- Japan (Sasebo, Tokyo, Yokohama, Yokosuka)
- Liberia
- Madagascar (Antananarivo, Marolambo)
- Malta
- Mozambique (Beira, Chimoio, Posto Campo)
- Puerto Rico
- Saipan
- Sicily (Palermo, Sigonella)
- Singapore
- South Africa
- South Korea (Chinhae)
- St. Croix
- St. Kitts & Nevis
- St. Vincent
- USA – (AL, AR, AZ, CA, DC, DE, FL, GA, HI, IL, IN, KY, LA, MA, MD, MS, NJ, NY, OH, PA, TN, TX, VA, WA)
- Zambia (Choma, Lusaka)
- Zimbabwe (Bulawyo, Gweru)

If you've enjoyed this book and it was a blessing to you, pass it on. Purchase another copy for someone else or send one to a military person you know.

FROM SAILOR TO SAINT

How I Found True Peace and Purpose

RANDRICK CHANCE

ALSO AVAILABLE NOW!

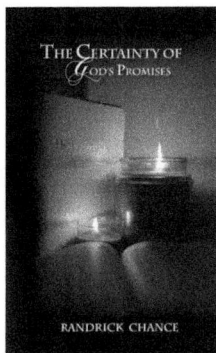

TCOGP - BK
Donation: $5.00

MP- MAG
Donation: $7.99

COMING SOON!

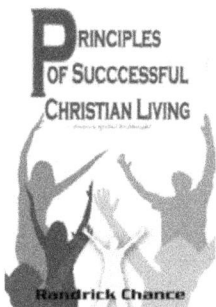

POSCL - BK
Donation: $14.99

LTLOF - BK
Donation: $7.00

MISSIONS RESOURCES
P.O. Box 11942
Huntsville, AL 35814
www.7SMR.org

I also encourage you to make a contribution to the National Association for the Prevention of Starvation (NAPS) to help many others find hope, peace, and relief. Give online at www.napsoc.org or mail your contributions to:

NAPS
Box 196
Oakwood University
Huntsville, AL 35896
256-726-7056

AOY-BK
Suggested Donation: $15.00

Available from NAPS

www.ingramcontent.com/pod-product-compliance
Lightning Source LLC
Chambersburg PA
CBHW072021040426
42447CB00009B/1678